RESIDENTIAL LANDSCAPING I

RESIDENTIAL
LANDSCAPING I

PLANNING/DESIGN/CONSTRUCTION

SECOND EDITION

THEODORE D. WALKER

Fellow, American Society of Landscape Architects

 VAN NOSTRAND REINHOLD
_____ New York

Library of Congress Catalog Card Number 89-21468
ISBN 0-442-23782-0

Printed in the United States of America

Van Nostrand Reinhold
115 Fifth Avenue
New York, New York 10003

Van Nostrand Reinhold International Company Limited
11 New Fetter Lane
London EC4P 4EE, England

Van Nostrand Reinhold
480 La Trobe Street
Melbourne, Victoria 3000, Australia

Nelson Canada
1120 Birchmount Road
Scarborough, Ontario M1K 5G4, Canada

16 15 14 13 12 11 10 9 8 7 6 5 4 3 2 1

Library of Congress Cataloging-in-Publication Data

Walker, Theodore D.
    Residential landscaping/Theodore D. Walker.—2nd ed.
        p.   cm.
    Includes bibliographical references.
    Contents: 1. Planning, design, construction.
    ISBN 0-442-23782-0 (v. 1)
    1. Landscape gardening.   2. Landscape architecture.   I. Title.
SB473.W34   1990
712.6—dc20   89-21468
                                                       CIP

Contents

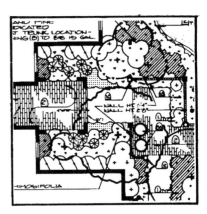

5 Construction Design 52

In a design setting the materials discussed in Chapter 4 are illustrated.

6 Planting Design 68

The process of designing with plants considering form, texture, color, line, variety, balance, and emphasis. Plant massing, transition and scale. The functional qualities of plants for visual control, physical barriers, shade, precipitation and humidity control, noise control, erosion control and wildlife habitats. Developing a plant list prior to design.

7 Construction Techniques

115

Creating such landscape features as paving, edgings, steps, walls, fences, decks, shelters, benches, pools, planters, play equipment, lighting and irrigation.

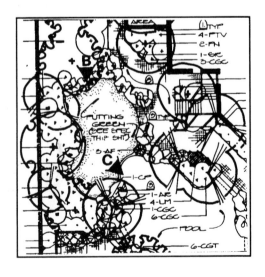

Why Landscape?

Landscaping, for the purposes of this book, can be defined as the physical improvement of a piece of property. That improvement could and should include more than plants. It means the best placement of the house on the site, orientation of the house for energy savings, screening for privacy, planning for passive and active recreation, and much more.

A well-landscaped residential site increases the value of the property and provides pleasant surroundings, certainly making a home easier to sell — an important consideration in today's mobile society.

Instead of just a patch of grass around the home, a shrub at each side of the front door and a tree or two scattered about, careful landscaping expands the living and play areas with patio areas, pools, walks, vegetable gardens, windbreaks, and game courts, enabling you to take full advantage of the outdoors when weather permits. With the increased cost of gasoline and other forms of energy, it makes sense to stay home and enjoy it. Another landscaping plus is growing your own fruits, vegetables, and herbs so you can save on inflationary food bills.

Fig. 1.1 A well-designed small site. Privacy is assured with the wall and fence. The backyard can be attractive without grass and offer a variety of activities such as dining, sitting, swimming and other recreation. Design by Theodore Brickman Co.

BEAUTY AND SECURITY

Landscaping adds attractiveness and a sense of aesthetics to a home, and improves the appearance of your community. When the neighborhood as a whole begins to think of landscaping, a certain pride emerges, as each owner creates and plans for individuality. Homes architecturally similar to many other houses in the same neighborhood can be highly individualized by the way they are landscaped.

Water used in the landscape provides dramatic aesthetic impact. Still water with water lilies or a reflecting pond can mirror the landscape beyond: the branching of trees, the sky and the clouds, and flowers. Moving water can duplicate the sound of a canyon stream; a splashing fountain can mask many highway noises. Splashing water also has psychological cooling effects which make people feel more comfortable, even though there may not be any significant change in the temperature. Moving water is a conversation piece and a focal point within a landscape design, and, when combined with works of art, such as sculpture, it becomes an integral part of the overall aesthetics. Fences, stairs, and walls will control pedestrian movement through the neighborhood, provide protection from trespassers, and prevent small children from wandering.

A home landscape that is well-designed and thoroughly planned also increases safety and security. Barrier planting can prevent intruders and increase privacy, and night lighting not only contributes to safety and security, it can also extend the hours the landscape can be used for entertaining and active recreation like volleyball and swimming.

When the family includes handicapped members landscaping should include ramps, handrails, and curb-cuts, and should avoid any barriers that will limit the handicapped individual's movement and enjoyment of the landscape.

Fig. 1.2 *Flat sites can be altered to increase their beauty. Mounding on this site created a rolling landscape with interesting shadow patterns in summer and pockets of snow in winter. Clumps of Bayberry break up the open space. Design by A. E. Bye and Associates.*

2

Fig. 1.3

Fig. 1.4

Fig. 1.5

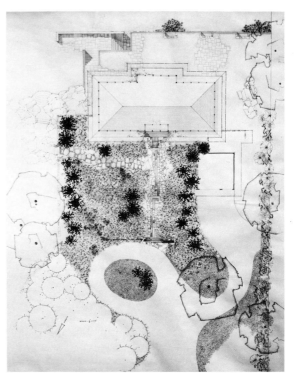

Fig. 1.6

Figures 1.3 - 1.6 *Low maintenance is the feature of this garden which is on a rocky site. Drought tolerant plants were used in place of grass. Stone walks harmonize with the rock outcroppings. Design by A. E. Bye and Associates.*

ENERGY SAVINGS

Careful landscaping can also enhance energy savings; for example, deciduous shade trees that shade your home in the summer between 10 in the morning and mid-afternoon (the hours of the most intense heat) can reduce the temperature in the home by several degrees. If your home is heavily insulated, the temperature rise is reduced considerably within the attic area. During the winter, deciduous trees provide almost no shade for the home, thus enabling the sun to pass through the tree branches and in turn help heat the home, thus providing significant savings in heating costs.

You should take into account the orientation of your home in relation to the sun and the location of the home's windows so the sun can penetrate in the winter but not in the summer. On the sides of the house exposed to the winter winds, you should have fewer windows and doors, and these windows should be smaller. In hot, sunny climates, west facings windows should be avoided.

Windbreaks are barriers that deflect the wind above and around the home, thus reducing the amount of heat carried away by the movement of wind against the home. Soil mounding, if carefully handled, can also do much the same thing. Sometimes you can create a more rapid or immediate effect by using both mounding and high plants to provide sufficient height to deflect the wind.

If you do not have enough room for big shade trees or mounds and windbreaks, consider using espaliered plants (plants grown flat against a wall). This green cover on the surface of the building shades the wall, and reduces the penetration of heat providing some energy savings and adding aesthetic qualities to the home.

During the planning phase consider energy-saving devices such as solar collectors and where they are to be placed. They can be located as part of the roof structure or placed next to the house if fully exposed to the sun.

Finally, energy can be saved by not planting a lawn. Instead, consider the use, especially on small sites, of ground covers, gravel mulches, or native plantings. In areas where irrigation is a necessity, such as the southwest, a gravel mulch in place of a lawn results in significant savings because water use is reduced. Water conservation is an increasing national concern.

RECREATION

The home is a good place for recreation; how much depends upon the amount of available space. There are two types of recreation — passive, which involves things like sitting, reading, sunbathing, and lounging; and active, which includes such things as hopscotch, basketball, volleyball, shuffleboard, croquet, and vigorous swimming. Usually the areas for passive recreation are located relatively close to the home as part of a patio or deck, but they can be designed to be a structure located away from the home, such as a playground or gazebo, where you can get away from the telephone and other demands of the home. For children's active recreation, manufactured swings, slides, and climbers are easy to buy and install. If you are interested in something different, you can buy or build contemporary wood play equipment, depending on your budget, time,

Fig. 1.7 *A low maintenance garden featuring grass, juniper and pine. The tall grass waves with the wind and its silvery color strongly contrasts against the dark greens of the pine and juniper. Design by A. E. Bye and Associates.*

Fig. 1.8

Fig. 1.9

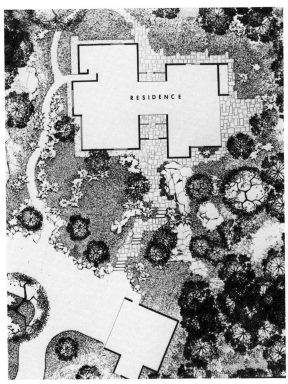

Fig. 1.10

Figures 1.8 - 1.10 *A low maintenance garden in a wooded setting. The home was sited for privacy and harmony with the existing woods. Native rock and shrubs were used to create the effect shown. There is no grass to mow. Designed by A. E. Bye and Associates.*

and interest. Such equipment is described later. For active teenagers, install basketball and volleyball facilities. Less strenuous activities like croquet and shuffleboard are for everyone; the equipment is easy to install.

People of all ages enjoy swimming because they can just sit or float in the water, or for more active people, dive and vigorously swim. Thus a pool can provide both active and passive recreation. A hot tub adjacent to the patio or deck is also a delightful form of recreation and relaxation.

Eating and drinking are other necessary and important adjuncts to recreation. Part of the eating may involve the process of cooking on the spot in a barbecue, whether charcoal, gas, or electric or a pit in which a fire can be started from wood.

OTHER ADVANTAGES

Plants add oxygen to the atmosphere, help reduce air and visual pollution, and control soil erosion. In addition to plants, mulches help hold water and return moisture into the subsoil, recharging the water tables, which is especially important in drought-prone areas or where water tables are dropping.

The manual labor needed for landscape development and maintenance provides healthy exercise and relaxation; many people find that gardening provides a release from everyday tensions and offers a creative and satisfying form of recreation.

The fragrance, color, shape, and form of shrubs, trees, or perennials and annuals add tremendous variety and interest to the garden. And the introduction of trees and shrubs into the environment provides a habitat and food source for various forms of wild life, including birds. There is also a certain delight in growing flowers and then cutting them for indoor decoration. Finally, growing certain kinds of flowers successfully can give you a sense of pride and satisfaction, and introduce you to the exotic aspects of gardening.

More and more families are using a portion of their landscape site for the production of food. The overriding reasons would appear to be financial, and as food costs continue to spiral upward, these reasons for gardening are becoming very real. However, people garden for many other reasons and these are just as important. Many believe the quality of home produced vegetables or fruits is superior to what can be purchased at the store. There is no question that produce picked at its prime in ripeness and not shipped is of superior quality. Some have a garden for recreational reasons. Caring for a garden provides exercise, and, as the produce is harvested, there is a satisfaction of seeing the results of one's hard work.

Fig. 1.11 In arid climates a low maintenance landscape can be designed using rock and native plants. Varying the size of the rock provides contrast in texture and a meandering line.

Fig. 1.12

Fig. 1.13

Fig. 1.14

Fig. 1.15

Figures 1.12 - 1.15 *Privacy and attractive living space can be designed for mobile homes. The increase in beauty will improve the resale value of the home as well as create a sense of individuality and permanence to a sometimes temporary living space. Design by Alex Pierce and Environment 21/E. A. Maddox.*

Fig. 1.16 Condominium projects can be designed to allow private landscaped living spaces for each owner. These spaces can be pre-designed and constructed, or left to the owner to develop to his/her own tastes. Design by Theodore Brickman Co.

Considerations

2

Before you can begin to design, several things must be considered, such as family needs, availability of materials, size of your property and soil conditions. If you carefully evaluate your needs, you will be much more successful and considerably more satisfied with the final results.

SELECTING AND EVALUATING A SITE

If you are planning to buy or rent a house and property, the following checklists are useful for selecting a potential site. First, consider the neighborhood and living conditions, and then evaluate the physical aspects of the property.

Medical Facilities. Does your family require a location close to emergency medical facilities? Is ambulance service readily available? How close is the nearest hospital? If you have pets, are there veterinary services nearby?

Fire and Police Protection. In many suburban areas there are enough fire and police stations to ensure protection for you and your family. But in outlying areas, rural communities, and some poorly-planned cities, fire and police stations may be few and far away. Do the stations have adequately trained personnel? Are the stations staffed with enough personnel?

Schools. Can your children walk to school, or will you have to drive them? Is there public transportation to the school, or does the school district provide busses? Do the schools have a good scholastic reputation?

Shopping. Close location to a grocery store and service stations may be more important to you than a major shopping center with many shops and products. Can you walk to stores, or will you have to drive?

Religious Facilities. The location of a church or synagogue may be important to you. If you visit such facilities regularly, a close location may be desirable and necessary to save transportation costs.

Public Transportation. Will you be able to get to work or shop by public transportation, or will you have to use your car? Does any public transportation run late at night or weekends?

Recreation. Are there playgrounds and spaces where children can play ball or pursue other activities? Can children bike to a swimming pool or to a larger park for basketball, tennis, volleyball, and so on? Are there any supervised recreational activities, such as Little League or Boy or Girl Scout troops? Are beaches and picnic areas nearby?

Utilities. A developed site will usually include water, sewer, electricity, storm drains and sometimes natural gas, sidewalks, curbs and gutters. But if the site is undeveloped, a sewage disposal system may have to be constructed or a well drilled, and this cost has to be included in your building budget. Moreover, extra charges may be required to secure power and telephone lines--some telephone companies charge mileage based on how far your home is from the central switching office.

Check with your local planning department for proposed highway plans. You may not want to locate near a future high speed road (freeway/expressway) where noise could be a problem. Conversely, the easy access of a new road may facilitate commuting to work.

Roads. Outside cities and suburban developments, good all-weather roads are important. Are access roads deeply rutted with mud or covered with snow drifts for lengthy periods? Is access from certain streets restricted? Is access permitted only under rigid conditions? If so, these factors may add considerable? If so, these factors may add considerable cost to the development of the home site. If your access road is lengthy and in an area of snowfalls, you may have to buy snow-removal equipment. Is the access road from a public road or street too steep, making it hazardous to maneuver vehicles in and out?

Neighborhood and Zoning Regulations. How do neighbors care for their homes and grounds? Pride is reflected by neatly, well-groomed sites and carefully maintained homes. Check local zoning regulations. Zoning is desirable because it protects the value of your property by providing orderly growth and preventing undesirable development. Familiarity with restrictions before construction will help you harmonize your development with the neighborhood and prevent unnecessary tensions. Generally the highest level of zoning restricts construction to single-family dwellings; other zoning prevents multifamily dwellings and commercial and industrial development. Certain areas of zoning might not permit a rental apartment as part of your site development. Does the local zoning protect you from the intrusion of commercial industrial activity that might cause noise or odors or disrupt a good view? Are there solar restrictions which affect the placement of trees which might shade a neighbor's solar unit? In a subdivision, is development further restricted beyond zoning by 'restrictive covenants?' These additional restrictions may determine such things as the minimum square footage you may build on one floor, maximum height of your roof line, architectural styles, height and placement of fences, placement of vertical and dish antennas, mailboxes, storage of boats and recreational vehicles, animals (including pets) and so on.

Topography. Is the lay of the land steep or flat; does it contain a depression or gully? The greater the change of topography on a site, the greater the care necessary to fit the house and landscape to it. Steep slopes are expensive to develop, requiring retaining walls to reduce erosion problems. Steep drives may be hard to use, especially in winter. Slopes with grass may be hard to mow and could be hazardous.

Soil. The quality of your soil is important if you want a garden. Many soils are heavy and poor, making it difficult to establish plants and hampering the use of on-site sewage disposal systems. A good, fertile topsoil is desirable as it already contains humus and nutrients needed to grow plants. You will have to arrange to have it stripped, stockpiled, and redistributed after construction. Contact your county agricultural agent (generally listed in the telephone directory) to find out about testing the soil.

Observe water tables and drainage patterns to know where the water runs to after a storm. A high water table during some seasons of the year may make a basement impractical. The drainage patterns have to be kept in mind as the site is developed to be sure that runoff is properly handled; water might accumulate in unexpected places after construction is done if you ignore drainage patterns.

Some soils will erode more than others during construction. Steep slopes may slip, resulting in slides during heavy rainfalls. Consult your local soil conservation service for help in these areas.

Vegetation. Check any existing vegetation on the site for quality. Good plants add to the value of a property. Many wooded sites sell at much higher prices because of the existing vegetation. If you are not familiar with plants, seek help from people at a nursery, a forester, or an extension horticulture agent, to identify the most dominant plants and to determine whether the plants should be saved. If plants on the site are to be saved, they will have to be located on a plan (see Chapter 3). Some areas may have restrictions on the removal and moving of native plants, or that new plantings may need to be compatible and follow certain prescribed guidelines. In certain arid areas plants may need to be used from a list which are known to use less water.

Size. Is there enough space on your home site? Check easements and setback lines with the local city or county engineer's office. (The information would also appear on a surveyor's plat.) These factors may reduce the buildable area of your lot considerably, leaving you with inadequate room for your home and other activities. Is off-street parking required in your area? (The amount of room needed for parking cars and the size of driveways is in Chapter 3.)

Glare and Reflected Light. Check for glare and light from nearby lakes and ponds and from adjacent light-colored paving or street lights. Many individuals discover that glare or reflected light increases their discomfort, and find it desirable to reduce it.

Views. Good views should be identified and preserved during the design phase. Unattractive views can be screened by fencing, plants, and walls. Is the site large? If so, views can be artificially created. Some directions on a site may be toward better views than others; identify these directions before the house is sited to take maximum advantage of potential views.

LOCATING THE HOME

If you have purchased a sizeable lot you will have considerable flexibility in the placement of the house on the site. The house need not be parallel or perpendicular to the property lines unless you find some compelling reason to do so. You may want to place the house in relation to views or in relation to the angle of the sun to take advantage of natural heating and cooling. On a large building site, locating the house on the highest portion has the advantages of providing better drainage in the case of a high water table and enabling you to have a basement. However, for unsheltered sites the highest elevation may also be subject to the greatest amount of wind. Winds help cool during the hot summer, but in cold winter they increase the discomfort. Wind problems can be somewhat modified by installing fences, barrier plantings, windbreaks, and mounding the earth.

If the site you selected is just large enough for your home, you may not have much flexibility in the placement of the house on the site. You should then try to harmonize the position of your house to the rest of the neighborhood.

The front entry should be readily identifiable and easily accessible to visitors. Off-street parking ideally should be away from the front of the house to avoid interfering with the appearance of the house. If the size of your lot is large enough, off-street parking can be accommodated very easily without intruding into the landscape. You can even screen it with plantings and moundings so it is relatively hidden. Any off-street parking should be convenient to the front entry of the house. On large-wooded sites the only means of entrance to the home is often the driveway itself. Thus the front entry to the house is not obvious to visitors until after they come down or go into the driveway and discover the house in its wooded setting. For privacy, you can develop a front courtyard that screens or otherwise shields the front entry of the house from view. The sense of entry can then be along the driveway, with the front entry of the house enclosed. In subdivisions with small lots and houses placed side by side, the narrow side yards between homes are difficult to use. In most instances these spaces become wastelands although most homeowners at least mow the lawn and maintain the area. However, with some imagination and creativity you can turn these spaces into useful areas; for example, fences can screen side yards from view, and a number of gardening or other kinds of activities can be connected into these narrow side yards.

FAMILY NEEDS

Whether you are buying or renting a site or just want to improve the one you have, all the needs of the family have to be considered. Begin by listing each member of the family and include age and sex; then, by each name list hobbies, favorite outdoor activities, and recreation. Just how many activities can be accommodated on your particular site is going to depend on the available space. You may have to rank by priority many things listed in the checklist and select those of higher priority, setting aside those that cannot be accommodated because of limited space. Most homeowners have needs that far exceed the site's space; you have to be flexible. The use of the outdoor area of your site can be broken down into any one of three potential uses: (1) general gardening, (2) entertainment, and (3) recreation.

General Gardening. Do you want minimum, moderate, or high maintenance? Minimum maintenance may require additional installation costs and precludes such items as vegetable gardens, annual and perennial flower beds, or anything requiring much time and/or manual labor.

Entertainment. Your family may like to entertain frequently. Will the groups be large or small, informal or formal? Is most the entertaining in the form of socializing? Is much of the socializing done indoors or outdoors, or a combination of both? Do you like to cook outdoors over a grill or pit? Is a swimming pool a desirable part of the entertaining pattern of the family? Does much of your entertaining occur at night where lighting might be critaical. The answers may dictate the amounts of paving material needed, the space devoted to entertainment activities, and the other facilities that may be needed to make the landscape complete and functional.

Recreation. As mentioned in Chapter 1, recreation generally is classified into two different types: active or passive. For the homeowner, active recreation includes such activities as badminton, croquet, tether ball, volleyball, basketball, or horseshoes. Some of these sports could be played on the lawn, but others, like shuffleboard or basketball, have to be played on a paved surface. Certain activities can take place close to the patio or the rear of the house, but others may have to be to the side, such as adjacent to the driveway.

Your landscape plan should provide areas for passive recreation, like: sitting, relaxing, sun tanning and reading.

After determining your family needs, one of the first things you need to do is establish priorities. Your site may not hold all the needs you feel your family has, so some will have to be eliminated. Or you may not be able to afford all of the things that you would like to do on your site; these features will have to be eliminated because of cost. What are your long-range plans for living in the home? Will you be there five years, ten years? Will you be transferred to another location? Would you build or buy a smaller home later, when the family has grown and left?

All these questions need to be considered and answered as part of your planning; as you establish your priorities and needs, take these questions and answers into account. For example, if you know that you are going to be transferred, you will want to have a finished landscape that can add to the resale value and shorten resale time. If you anticipate being on your site permanently, you can begin to develop long-range plans that provide you a year-by-year implementation schedule whereby the garden and recreation areas are created as your budget allows.

Patio/Deck. Sometimes a low wood deck can be combined with harder paved materials to form a patio area. The size of this area will depend upon your family's needs and activities. A wood deck is immediately usable after a storm because it generally dries off very quickly. Patio paving materials include concrete, exposed aggregate concrete, brick, stone, asphalt, precast patio stones, and wood blocks. The patio and/or deck should be easily accessible from the dining or living room or a family room.

Some type of seating is desirable for patios: permanently built benches, seat-high walls or planters, or movable tables and chairs. If you want shade, existing trees may provide enough. On new, open sites, build overhead roofs, install vine covered trellises, or consider table umbrellas.

For family outdoor cooking equipment, consider such possibilities as a barbecue pit, a portable grill, or a permanent gas or charcoal grill. Convenient access should be provided from the kitchen or dining room. Additional amenities such as running water, sinks, and multiple electrical outlets may be necessary if you will be doing much outdoor cooking.

If the patio/deck will be for 'passive' living the area should be an extension of the interior home living areas. You could have two levels of patios or two levels of decks, one level for dining and the other for living purposes, with the levels perhaps joined and the view then focusing on one or more portions of the landscaped garden and distant view. If you prefer to move activities completely away from the house, consider building a gazebo. This can be located so it can be seen from the house, or it may

be completely enclosed or excluded from view. A secluded gazebo will provide escape from the telephone and other annoyances.

Water. Water can be still, ornamental pools, including reflecting pools, pools for water lilies and other decorative water plants, and pools for fish, or moving–water from a jet or water cascading from one level to another level. Many people find the sound of water very appealing. Swimming pools come in many sizes and shapes. Keep in mind your budget, local legal requirements, costs of liability insurance, and increased maintenance problems.

Fences. You can ensure privacy by installing a fence. Simple wire fences will prevent physical intrusion but will provide no visual privacy. Wire fences usually start at heights of 3 feet and go to full heights of 6 or more feet. Fences can also be constructed of metal, wood, or plastic panels. Solid walls of brick, stone, or concrete block will also ensure visual privacy as well as reduce unwanted sound.

Lighting. The amount of lighting will depend upon the use of the site and cost. Lighting can be both functional and aesthetic. Aesthetic lighting is placed in such a manner as to hid the source of the light; only reflected light can be seen. Functional lighting includes the kind used to illuminate sports and other active games and steps and walks during the evening hours. It also includes lights strategically placed for security, to reduce the risk of criminal instrusion. There are numerous lighting fixtures on the market for a variety of purposes; a complete discussion is included in Chapter 7.

Children's Play Areas. If a neighborhood playground for small children is not readily available or safe, you may want to add certain play facilities as part of the landscape design: a sandbox, swing, slide, wading pool, play house or tree house, and so on. The playground should be situated so that children can be watched from the kitchen or other high activity areas of the house, yet separated a bit from the more quiet activity areas of the landscape.

Flower and Vegetable Gardens. Keep in mind that maintaining flower and vegetable gardens is time consuming. You should include these in your landscape design only if you love gardening and pursue it as a hobby, form of recreation, or means of food production to reduce the family budget. You may then also want cold frames for early starting of plants, a compost pit, a greenhouse, and an area for bulbs and herbs. A vegetable or cut-flower garden should not be within the more furnished landscape area of the lot or site; it should be to one side, perhaps screened from view, with ready access to the kitchen or utility area of the house.

Service Areas. This category includes dog houses, dog runs, or other pet requirements; clotheslines; storage shelters or space for recreation vehicles like campers, boats, or trailers or for lawn and garden equipment (like mowers, sprinklers, hoses, sprayers, fertilizer spreaders, peat moss, garden tools, patio furniture); bird feeders and bird houses; and trash containers. These facilities should be relatively close to the garage or home for convenience. A dog run should be isolated unless you want it within view so you can observe the dog from time to time.

Irrigation Systems. In those parts of the country where additional irrigation is needed during certain seasons of the year to supplement natural rainfall, the installation of an irrigation system may reduce the time involved in hand watering and ensure adequate moisture for plant growth.

Once you complete the checklist, and you feel your assessment sufficiently represents the needs of your family, you should utilize it in the preparation of your own plan (Chapter 3) or give it to a landscape architect you have hired to prepare your landscape design.

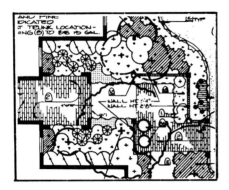

Preparing Plans

3

This chapter provides some help if you want to design your own plans. Note, however, that it does not contain *all* the answers because each site is so different, and there is not enough room in this book to cover such a variety. If you want to avoid costly mistakes and do the best work, plans must be prepared before you tackle any major construction or remodel the grounds around the home, including a driveway.

There are four basic landscape design styles. Residential gardens are infrequently designed in the formal style, called *symmetrical* balance because both sides are equal along a central axis. (see Fig. 3.1) A few formal gardens have been preserved within the United States to remind us of the styles of the past; such gardens are costly to maintain and were always intended to be looked at rather than lived in. Modern living demands a more informal environment, and this includes the design of the landscaping. The placement of trees and shrubs, sidewalks, patios, pools and fountains, play areas, and so forth is seldom along a central axis or equally spaced or placed in the landscape. Now they are placed according to their best functional relationships creating an informal (*asymmetrical*) design.

The informal landscape plan can be rectangular or *modular* — all intersecting paving, grass areas, sidewalks, and other lines are at right angles to each other — or *circular or curved* lines (free-form style). (Figures 3.2 to 3.3)

A third style, *angular*, utilizes straight lines which intersect each other at varying angles, and the

Fig. 3.1 *Formal design style, symmetrical.*

Fig. 3.2 *Modular design style. Design by Theodore Brickman Co.*

final style is *naturalistic*: the entire landscape is without defined lines or forms, such as the landscape of a heavily wooded site in which nature is not basically modified. (Figures 3.4 to 3.5)

The easiest design style for the novice homeowner to work with is the modular, while circular and angular styles are much more difficult to handle and perfect. The naturalistic style also needs to be handled with extreme sensitivity to ensure harmony between the structure or home and the surrounding natural environment that can easily deteriorate through abuse or overuse. A basic understanding of plant ecology is necessary to succeed, and you must be willing to tolerate the more unkempt appearance of a natural landscape if you want this style.

Fig. 3.3 *Free-form design style, curved lines, asymmetrical balance.*

Fig. 3.5 *Naturalistic design style. Design by A. E. Bye and Associates.*

Fig. 3.4 *Angular design style. Design by Edward D. Stone, Jr. and Associates.*

PROPERTY PLAN

The first plan to prepare is one that locates the property lines in relationship to the home and any other existing features, such as trees or clumps of vegetation, utility poles, walks, buildings, and driveways. Most owners of new homes will generally have access to a plan that shows the house as it relates to the property lines, with the lengths and direction of each property line shown; it is then fairly easy to add to that particular plan. If you own an older home, you may have a little more difficulty trying to establish the size of the house and its relationship to the property lines. An easy way to do this is to work with blue-lined graph paper. Use the type where eight squares 1 inch or 1/8 inch (one square) equals 1 foot for a reduced scale drawing. (Fig. 3.6)

Lay out the house and the site on the graph paper. First locate the house. Measure the length of each side of the house and the placement of the windows and doors (accurately to within one inch); indicate these dimensions on the paper. Then measure from the house to the property lines and place these measurements on the paper. If property lines run at angles to the house, take several measurements parallel and perpendicular to the various sides and corners of the house to establish the exact location of the property line in relation to the house. This technique can also be used to locate trees, walls, and other existing features. (Fig. 3.7)

There are two techniques for measuring changes of slope if the slope is gentle, without a lot of changes. (1) use a long, straight 2 x 4 on edge with a spirit level, or (2) use a hand level and a rod. (Fig. 3.8) If there is considerable change of grade or the grade or the grade becomes complicated in its character (ravines and so on), you should hire a professional surveyor.

Fig. 3.6 *Graph paper is available in various size sheets.*

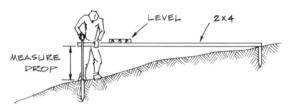

STAKES MAY BE USED AS REFERENCE POINTS. UNIFORM PLACEMENT AT RIGHT ANGLE TO A CORNER OF THE HOUSE WILL PROVIDE AN ACCURATE MAP OF SLOPES.

Fig. 3.8 *Technique for measuring elevation changes.*

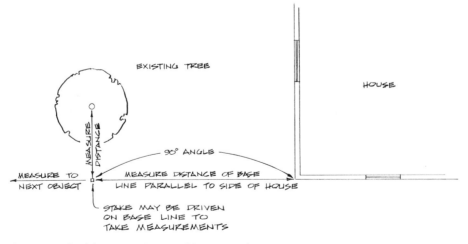

Fig. 3.7 *Method for measuring an object on a site.*

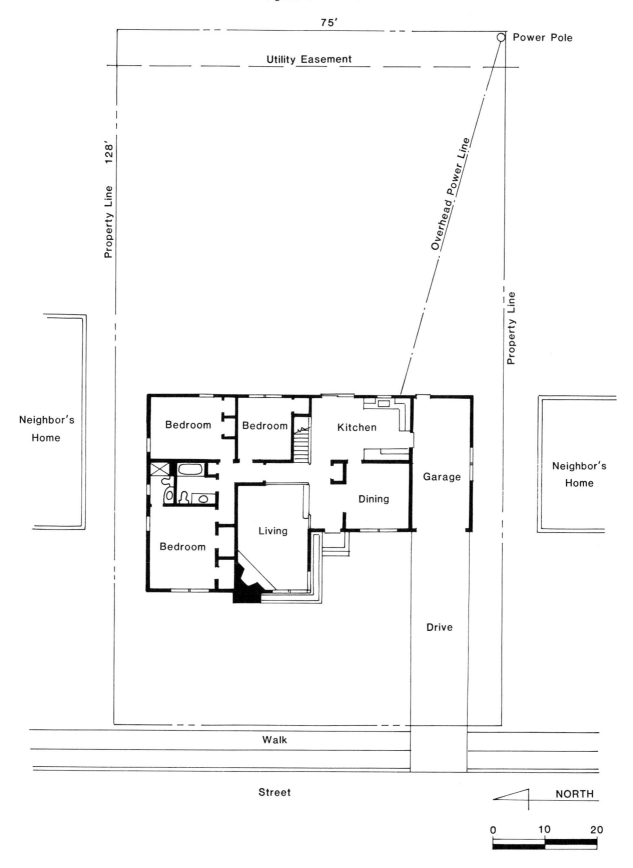

Fig. 3.9 *Example of a property plan for a small lot.*

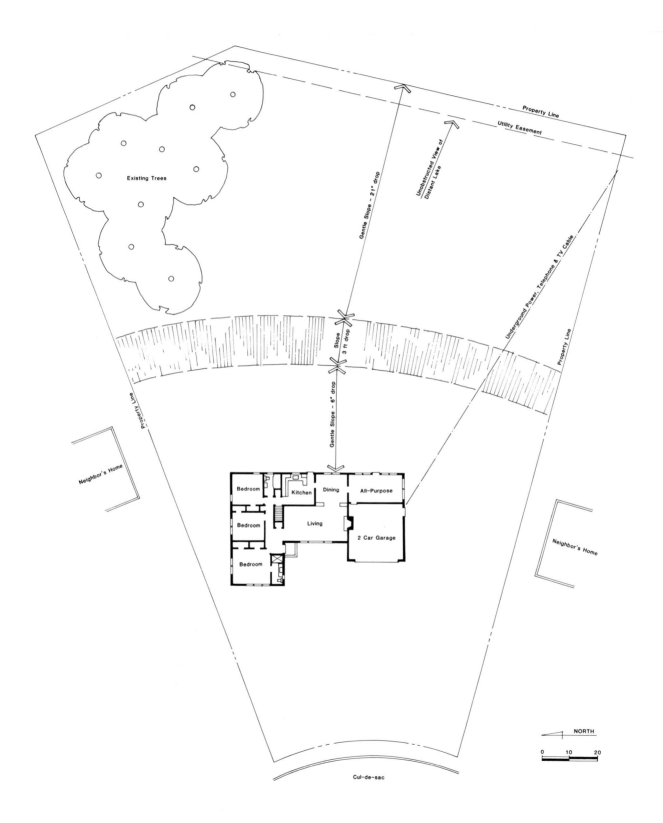

Labels within the figure:

Existing Trees

Property Line

Utility Easement

Gentle Slope – 21" drop

Unobstructed View of Distant Lake

Underground Power, Telephone & TV Cable

Property Line

Slope 3 ft drop

Gentle Slope – 6" drop

Property Line

Neighbor's Home

Bedroom
Bedroom
Bedroom
Kitchen
Living
Dining
All-Purpose
2 Car Garage

Neighbor's Home

NORTH

0   10   20

Cul-de-sac

Fig. 3.10 *Example of a property plan for a large lot.*

BUBBLE DIAGRAM

Once the house and grounds an all the existing features are on plan, you can begin to study any additions that are to be made to the site. First, review the checklists of needs you assembled (as described in Chapter 2). Based upon these checklists, establish a rough bubble diagram of use relationships on a piece of lightweight sketching tissue (transparent paper that lets the property plan show through) laid over the plan. With this bubble diagram it is possible to make several studies showing how various elements can relate to each other.

More slowly and carefully, thinking out each alternation, and then let the plan set for the few days. Come back and reevaluate what you have done. Letting time elapse provides you with a much better idea of the alternatives as they are developed. As you study the bubble diagram, also consider such things as the angle of the sun in the summer and winter and what effect it might have on certain windows or areas that need to be shaded. Are there views that need to be opened up, enhanced, or accentuated?

When establishing your use relationships, also consider circulation patterns, how to get people in and out of the various areas of your home, views for watching any children playing, and screening of unsightly areas. Is there easy access from the driveway to the backyard for moving wheelbarrows, lawn mowers, or other gardening equipment? Study all these factors carefully prior to final design. For examples, see Figures 3.11 and 3.12.

USE FACILITIES

The next step after selecting the final bubble diagram is to determined the more precise sizes and shapes of use facilities. You need to be aware of certain minimum sizes for use and comfort. For example, patios that are too small may not hold a picnic table and chairs and permit people to circulate around all these items, especially when the grass is wet and no one wants to move off the patio. Sidewalks which are too narrow are difficult to walk

Table 3.1 Game and Sports Areas

NAME	DIMENSIONS OF PLAY AREAS	USE DIMENSIONS	SPACE REQUIRED (SQ. FT.)	NUMBER OF PLAYERS
Badminton	17' x 44' single	25' x 60'	1,500	2
	20' x 44' double	30' x 60'	1,800	4
Baseball	75' x 82' diamond	250' x 250'	62,500	18
Basketball	35' x 60'	50' x 75'	3,750	10-12
Clock Golf	circle: 20'-40' in dia.	30' circle	706	any no. (4-8)
Croquet	30' x 60'	30' x 60'	1,800	any no. (4-8)
Field Hockey	120' x 200'	150' x 250'	37,500	22
Handball	20' x 30'	30' x 35'	1,050	2 or 4
Hopscotch	2' x 12½'	10' x 20'	200	2-10
Horseshoe Pitching	stakes 25' apart	15' x 40'	600	2 or 4
Paddle Tennis	18' x 39'	30' x 60'	1,800	2 or 4
Shuffleboard	6' x 52'	10' x 64'	640	2 or 4
Soccer	100' x 200'	125' x 240'	30,000	22
Softball	45' diamond	150' x 150'	22,500	20
Swimming Pool	14' x 28'	20' x 40'	800	1-10
Table Tennis	5' x 9'	12' x 20'	240	2 or 4
Team Dodgeball	circle: 40' boys'	60' x 60'	3,600	20
	35' girls'	50' x 50'	2,500	20
Tennis	27' x 78' single	60' x 120'	7,200	2 or 4
	36' x 78' double			
Tether Tennis	circle: 6' dia.	20' x 20'	400	2
Touch Football	120' x 240'	140' x 280'	39,200	22
Volleyball	25' x 50'	40' x 70'	2,800	12-16

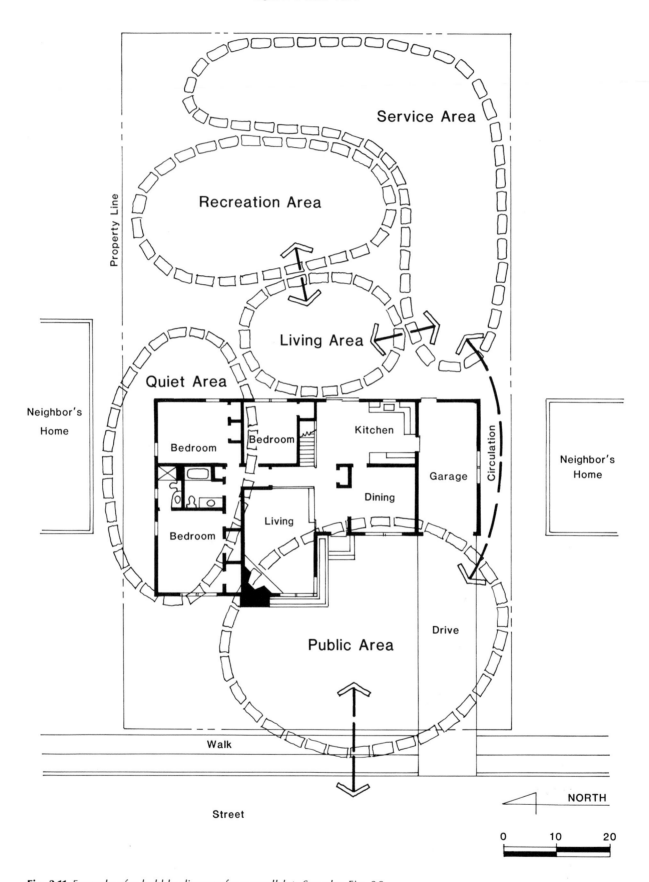

Fig. 3.11 *Example of a bubble diagram for a small lot. See also Fig. 3.9.*

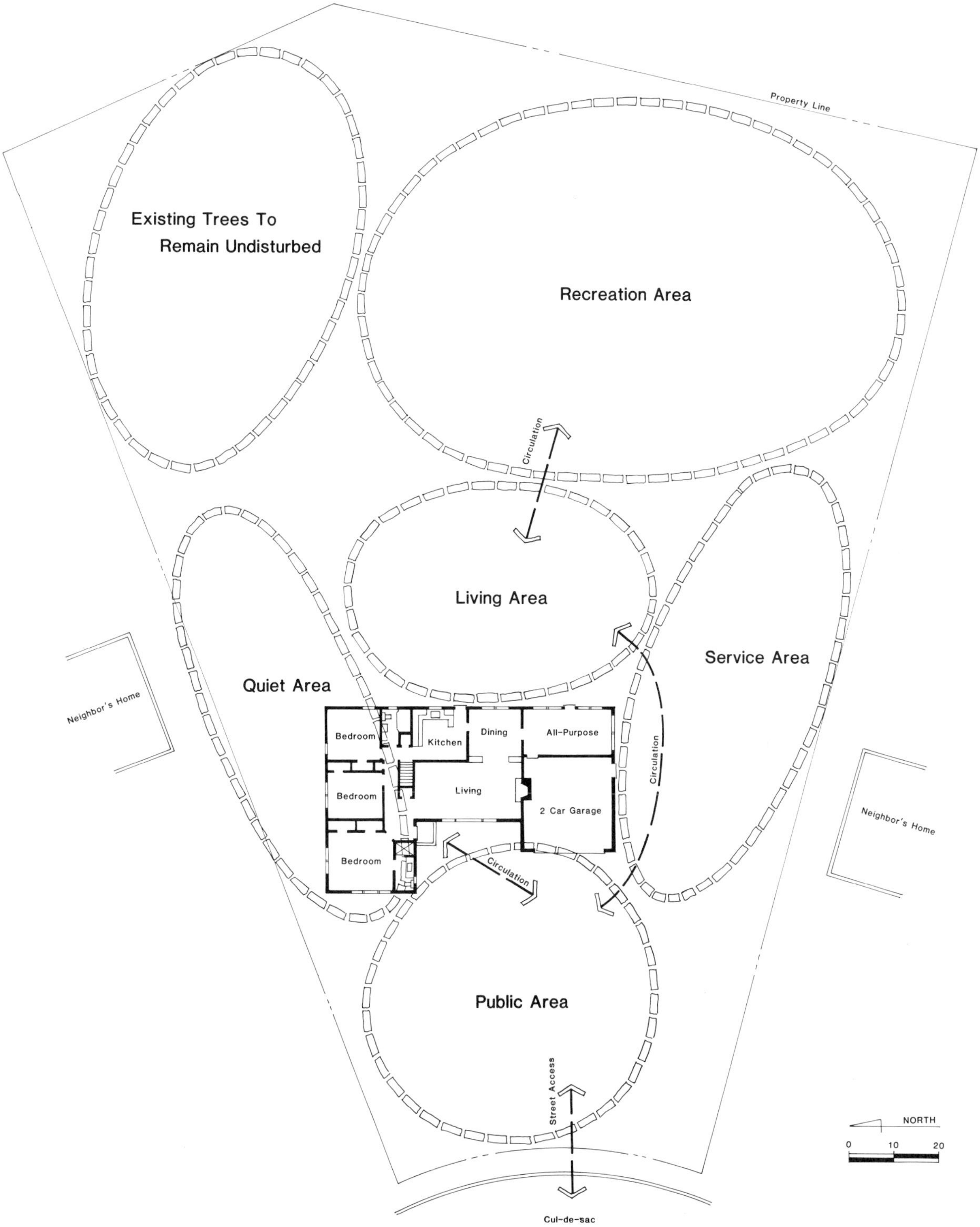
Property Line
Existing Trees To
Remain Undisturbed
Recreation Area
Circulation
Living Area
Service Area
Quiet Area
Neighbor's Home
Bedroom
Kitchen
Dining
All-Purpose
Bedroom
Living
2 Car Garage
Bedroom
Circulation
Circulation
Neighbor's Home
Public Area
Street Access
NORTH
0
10
20
Cul-de-sac

Fig. 3.12 *Example of a bubble diagram for a large lot. See also Fig. 3.10.*

on comfortably; two people side by side need approximately 4 feet on a sidewalk. If a garden gate is less than 36 inches wide, it is very difficult to push a wheelbarrow through it. Consider leg room around permanently installed benches. Have sufficient room around a swimming pool so there can be circulation as well as sunbathing: minimum of 3 feet for just circulating and 6 feet for circulation and sunbathing parallel to the pool. Is there enough room between a swing and a fence so children will not bump it when they are swinging? Careful consider all these subtle factors before your plans are final.

PRE-DESIGN

If you have access to video imaging hardware and software, it is possible to evaluate the design possiblities before committing your ideas to paper. Because of the tremendous flexibility of the computer it is thus possible to experiment with arrangements and design forms long before the construction begins. (Figures 3.16 to 3.17)

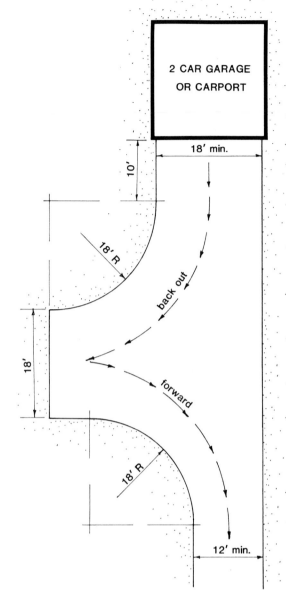

Fig. 3.14 *Dimensions for a 'Y' drive.*

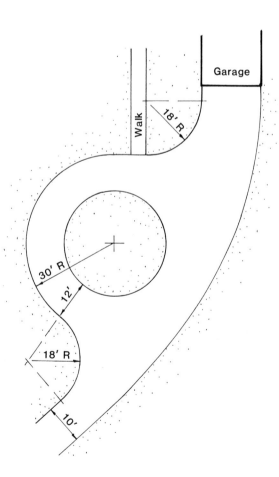

Fig. 3.13 *Dimensions for a circle drive.*

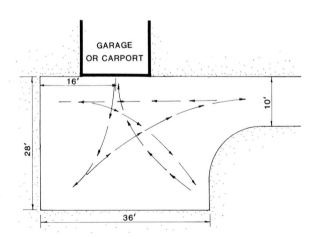

Fig. 3.15 *Dimensions for a double 'Y' drive.*

22

Fig. 3.16 *Video image of a home before designing begins. Courtesy of New Image Industries, Inc.*

Fig. 3.17 *Video image of the same home as in Fig. 3.16 with pool, paving and plants added. Courtesy of New Image Industries, Inc.*

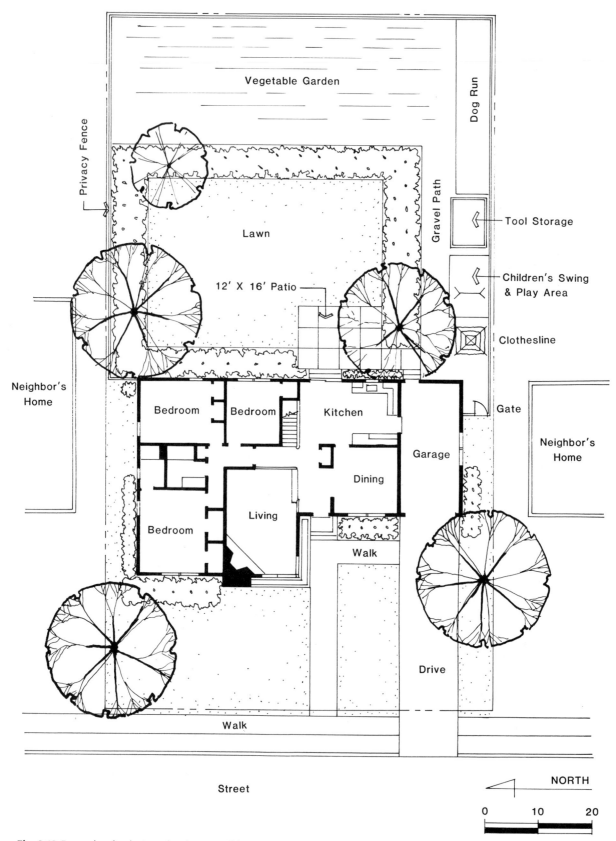

Neighbor's Rear Yard

Vegetable Garden

Dog Run

Privacy Fence

Gravel Path

Tool Storage

Lawn

Children's Swing & Play Area

12' X 16' Patio

Clothesline

Neighbor's Home

Bedroom

Bedroom

Kitchen

Gate

Neighbor's Home

Garage

Living

Dining

Bedroom

Walk

Drive

Walk

Street

NORTH

0   10   20

Fig. 3.18 *Example of a design plan for a small lot using the modular style of design. See also Figures 3.9 and 3.11.*

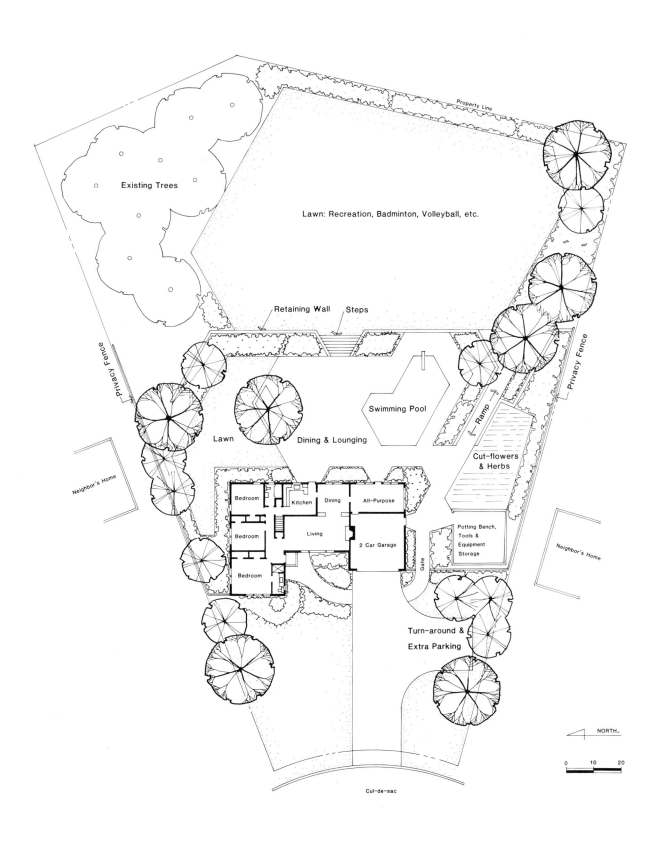

Existing Trees

Lawn: Recreation, Badminton, Volleyball, etc.

Property Line

Retaining Wall   Steps

Privacy Fence

Privacy Fence

Neighbor's Home

Swimming Pool

Lawn

Dining & Lounging

Ramp

Cut-flowers
& Herbs

Bedroom

Kitchen

Dining

All-Purpose

Living

2 Car Garage

Potting Bench,
Tools &
Equipment
Storage

Neighbor's Home

Bedroom

Bedroom

Gate

Turn-around &
Extra Parking

NORTH

0   10   20

Cul-de-sac

Fig. 3.19 *Example of a design plan for a large lot using the angular style of design.*
See also Figures 3.10 and 3.12.

DRAINAGE PATTERNS

After establishing the additions to your design, evaluate drainage. Where will the water go during a rainfall? Will it be able to drain away? Look at slopes. Paved areas should slope no less than 1/8 inch in 1 foot, draining away from any building. Planting and grass areas should slope 1/4 inch vertically for every foot of horizontal distance. (For more information on slopes, see Chapter 7)

Slopes should not be too steep. Grass areas should not be sloped greater than 1 foot vertically in every 3 feet of horizontal distance; anything steeper than that is difficult and dangerous to mow and could result in a hazardous situation. Where ground covers are used, the slope can be as steep as 1 foot vertical for every 2 feet of horizontal distance. If slopes need to be steeper than this, consider installing stone riprap or terraced retaining walls. Sidewalks can be as steep as 1-foot vertical rise in every 5-foot horizontal distance; if wheelchairs will be used on the slope, 1 foot in every 12 feet of horizontal distance is the maximum.

Pavement for tennis, basketball, or other play areas should be fairly flat, sloping 6 inches vertically in every 100 feet. If the slope is in excess of this, the pavement is uncomfortable to play on because the balls roll away from players much too rapidly.

LAYOUT AND STAKING PLANS

This plan contains the dimensions and sizes of everything that goes on the site. On this plan you carefully work out the exact size of each item and how it is fitting together with everything else. Also, at this stage give careful consideration to making sure that everything will fit and relate well to each other. After this is done, study the individual details of each and every item to be built, determining thickness and sizes and amounts of the individual construction schedule. (Figures 3.20 to 3.23) The schedule should begin with those items that require equipment to be brought in and end with the last item to be built, such as a fence that will enclose the area and prevent further access to the backyard. In many instances the

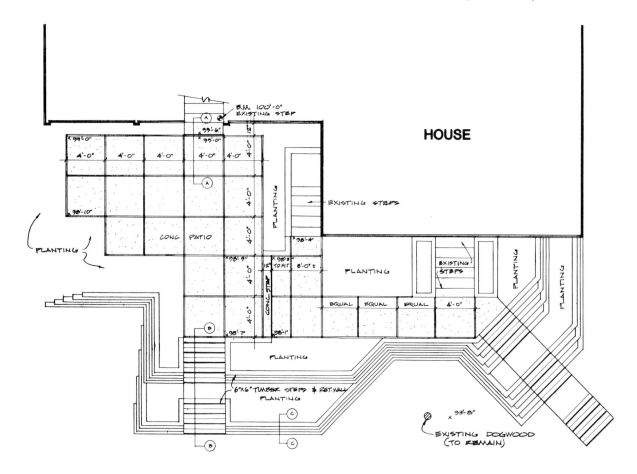

LAYOUT PLAN

Fig. 3.20 Example of a layout plan for a patio, steps, retaining wall and planting areas. Drainage patterns are identified by an 'x' followed by a number.

planting is the last thing to be done, unless there are some large trees that need to be moved in with cranes or large equipment. In this case most trees and large plants can be installed even before the paving and fences, with the smaller shrubs planted last.

PREPARING THE PLANTING PLAN

After the layout plan is completed, develop the planting plan by again using light sketching tissue and developing several alternatives, studying the principles of planting design as discussed in Chapter 6. You will also want to refer to the list of plants you assembled from the list of suggestions given to you in the same chapter. Decide where trees, shrubs, groups of vines or ground covers, and so on are to be placed and designate areas for flowers; label this information on the plan. Give careful attention to the proper sizes and spacing of plant materials. Identify the quantities on the plan with the name of the plant so at placement time plants can be put in quickly and easily with the least amount of time. The many different kinds of plants and the different kinds of hard materials used in a landscape plan are usually identified by different kinds of graphic symbols. Learn them and use them—they will save you much time.

Also consider energy conservation. Does your planting plan shade the house during the hottest part of the day to minimize air conditioning? Are prevailing winds able to create natural ventilation without being blocked by fences or screen planting? Are cold winter winds diverted with a windbreak? Indicate any energy conservation items on the plan.

After completing your plans you will probably want to prepare a cost estimate of the project. First make a list of all the materials you plan to use in the project. Such a list may need to include any tools you will have to buy or rent. Do not forget those small items like nails, mulches, and so on. Then, contact local suppliers for prices and make a computation of the total cost.

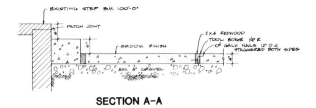

SECTION A-A

Fig. 3.22 *Paving detail. See 'A-A' on layout plan, Figure 3.20.*

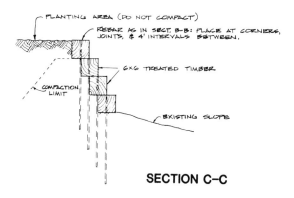

SECTION C-C

Fig. 3.23 *Retaining wall detail. See 'C-C' on layout plan, Figure 3.20.*

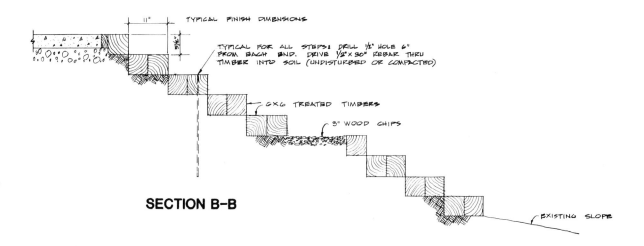

SECTION B-B

Fig. 3.21 *Detail of steps. See 'B-B' on layout plan, Figure 3.20.*

SOME DESIGN EXAMPLES

The remainder of this chapter is devoted to three design examples–residences designed by professional landscape architects which may provide a source of ideas and inspiration for quality design. The design style for each is different. Plans and photographs are provided for all three. On each plan the photographic view is noted with an arrow and bold letter.

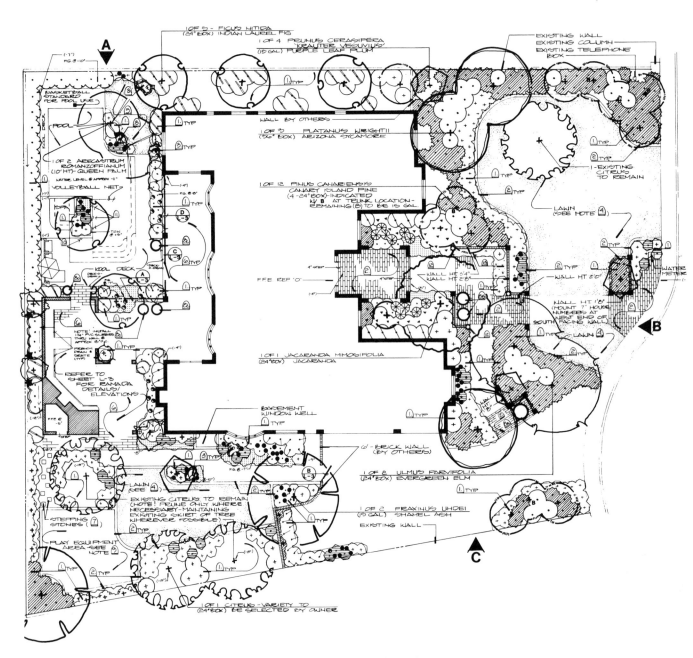

Fig. 3.24 Planting plan for Residence #1. The key to the plants can be found by looking at Fig. 3.25. Three photographic views can be examined by looking at Figures 3.29 to 3.31. Design by McConaghie/Batt and Associates.

PLANT KEY

CONTRACTOR RESPONSIBLE FOR VERIFYING PLANT COUNTS ON LANDSCAPE PLAN.

SYM	BOTANICAL NAME (COMMON NAME)	QUAN	SIZE
⊙	ASPARAGUS DENSIFLORUS 'MYERS' (MYERS ASPARAGUS)	3	1 GAL
⊙	ASPARAGUS DENSIFLORUS 'SPRENGERI' (SPRENGER ASPARAGUS)	48	1 GAL
	BOUGAINVILLEA 'SAN DIEGO RED' (BOUGAINVILLEA)	2	5 GAL
⊕	CARISSA GRANDIFLORA 'GREEN CARPET' (GREEN CARPET NATAL PLUM)	136	5 GAL
⊘	CARISSA GRANDIFLORA 'TUTTLEI' (TUTTLE NATAL PLUM)	17	5 GAL
	CYCUS REVOLUTA (SAGO PALM)	4	15 GAL
★	FICUS PUMILA (CREEPING FIG VINE)	3	1 GAL
	GARDENIA JASMINOIDES 'VEITCHII' (GARDENIA)	4	5 GAL
●	HEMEROCALLIS HYBRID (COMMON ORANGE DAYLILY)	52	1 GAL
	JUNIPERUS CHINENSIS 'MINT JULEP' (MINT JULEP JUNIPER)	136	5 GAL
⊙	LANTANA CAMARA 'CHRISTINE' (BUSH LANTANA)	26	1 GAL
	LANTANA MONTEVIDENSIS (TRAILING LANTANA)	30	1 GAL
●	MORAEA IRIDIODES (FORTNIGHT LILY)	18	1 GAL
⊘	NANDINA DOMESTICA (HEAVENLY BAMBOO)	12	5 GAL

SYM	BOTANICAL NAME (COMMON NAME)	QUAN	SIZE
	PYRUS KAWAKAMII (ESPALIERED EVERGREEN PEAR)	10	15 GAL
⊕	PHOENIX ROEBELENII (PIGMY DATE PALM)	4	15 GAL
⊘	PHILODENDRON SELLOUM (PHILODENDRON)	3	15 GAL
⊕	PITTOSPORUM TOBIRA 'VARIEGATA' (VARIGATED PITTOSPORUM)	19	5 GAL
◔	PITTOSPORUM TOBIRA 'WHEELERI' (WHEELERS DWARF PITTOSPORUM)	26	5 GAL
⊙	RAPHIOLEPIS INDICA 'BILL EVANS' (INDIAN HAWTHORN)	7	5 GAL
⊘	RAPHIOLEPIS INDICA 'PINK LADY' (INDIAN HAWTHORN)	30	5 GAL
⊛	STRELITZIA REGINAE (BIRD OF PARADISE)	11	15 GAL
⊕	STRELITZIA NICOLAI (GIANT BIRD OF PARADISE)	1	15 GAL
⊕	WISTERIA FLORIBUNDA 'ROSEA' (WISTERIA)	1	5 GAL
	XYLOSMA CONGESTUM (SHINY XYLOSMA)	19	5 GAL
	MYOPORUM PARVIFOLIUM (MYOPORUM) —PLANT 1' O.C.—	103	1 GAL

Fig. 3.25 *Key to the plants shown in Fig. 3.24*

Fig. 3.26 *Detail for planting and staking a tree.*

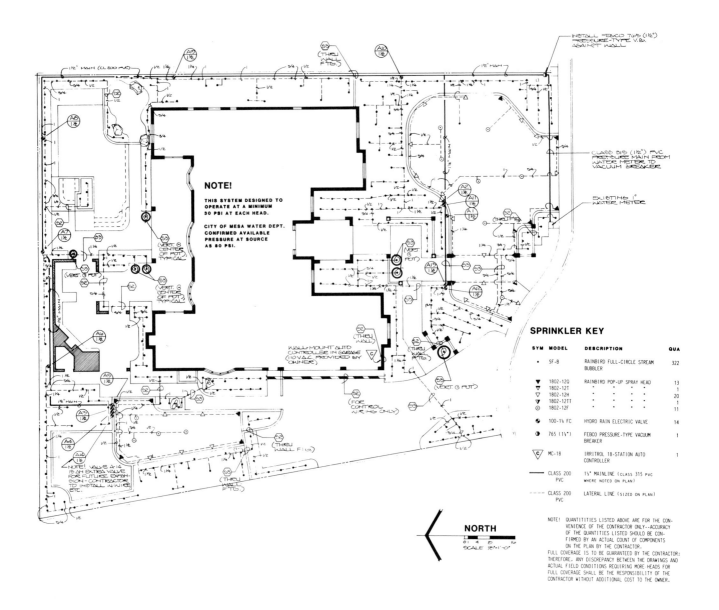

SPRINKLER KEY

SYM	MODEL	DESCRIPTION	QUA
•	5F-B	RAINBIRD FULL-CIRCLE STREAM BUBBLER	322
▼	1802-12Q	RAINBIRD POP-UP SPRAY HEAD	13
▽	1802-12T	" " " "	1
▽	1802-12H	" " " "	20
▼	1802-12TT	" " " "	1
⊙	1802-12F	" " " "	11
⬡	100-1½ FC	HYDRO RAIN ELECTRIC VALVE	14
◑	765 (1½")	FEBCO PRESSURE-TYPE VACUUM BREAKER	1
⬡C	MC-18	IRRITROL 18-STATION AUTO CONTROLLER	1
—— CLASS 200 PVC		1½" MAINLINE (CLASS 315 PVC WHERE NOTED ON PLAN)	
- - - CLASS 200 PVC		LATERAL LINE (SIZED ON PLAN)	

NOTE! QUANTITITLIES LISTED ABOVE ARE FOR THE CON-
VENIENCE OF THE CONTRACTOR ONLY—ACCURACY
OF THE QUANTITIES LISTED SHOULD BE CON-
FIRMED BY AN ACTUAL COUNT OF COMPONENTS
ON THE PLAN BY THE CONTRACTOR.
FULL COVERAGE IS TO BE GUARANTEED BY THE CONTRACTOR;
THEREFORE, ANY DISCREPANCY BETWEEN THE DRAWINGS AND
ACTUAL FIELD CONDITIONS REQUIRING MORE HEADS FOR
FULL COVERAGE SHALL BE THE RESPONSIBILITY OF THE
CONTRACTOR WITHOUT ADDITIONAL COST TO THE OWNER.

NORTH

0 1 4 8   16
SCALE ⅛"=1'-0"

Fig. 3.27 *Irrigation plan for Residence #1.*

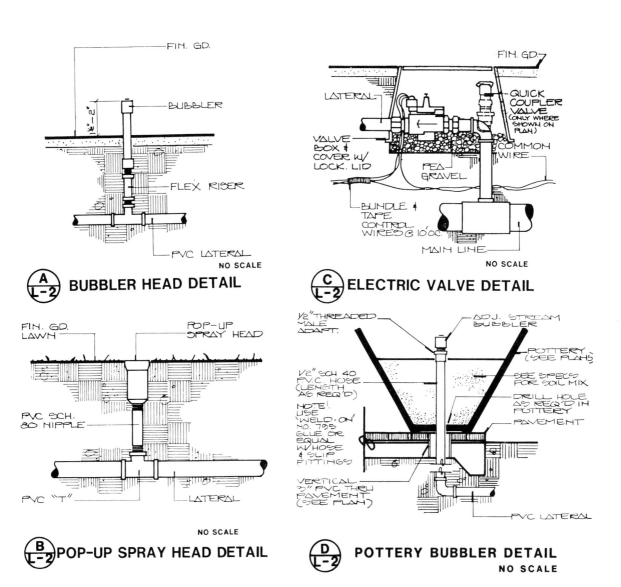

Fig. 3.28 *Details for the irrigation plan, Fig. 3.27.*

Fig. 3.29 *View A of Residence #1. The swimming pool area which is completely enclosed by a wall and separated from the home by a metal fence, a recommended safety feature. In the left foreground is a putting green and the building in the background provides shelter from the weather and cooking facilities.*

Fig. 3.30 *View B of Residence #1. This is the front entrance to the home.*

Fig. 3.31 *View C of Residence #1. An entrance from the driveway to the front door.*

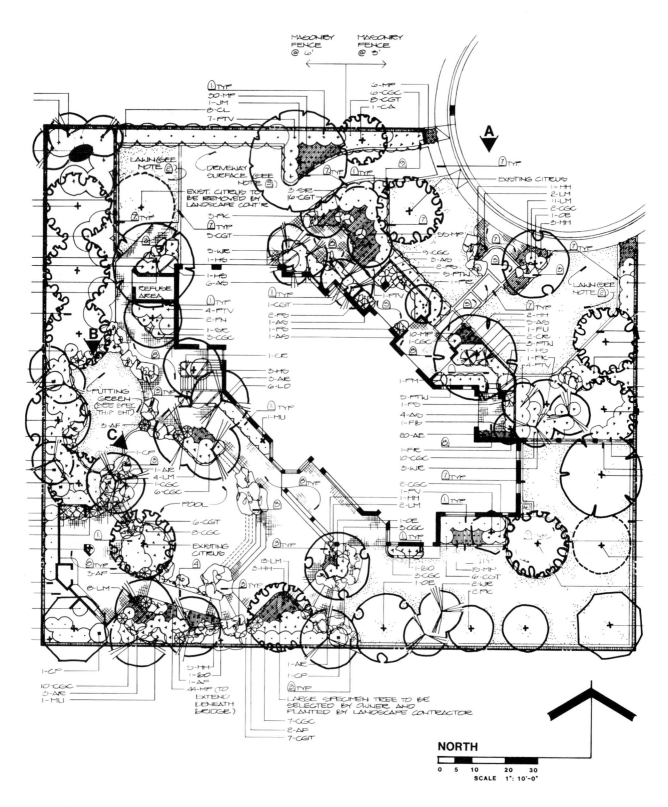

Fig. 3.32 *Plan for Residence #2. See Figures 3.33 to 3.35 for three photographic views. Design by McConaghie/Batt and Associates.*

Fig. 3.33 *View A for Residence #2. Front entrance of the home.*

Fig. 3.34 *View B for Residence #2. A putting green is in the foreground and a shelter with cooking facilities occupies the rear.*

Fig. 3.35 *View C for Residence #2. Swimming pool and patio with rear of home on the left. Rocks are man-made.*

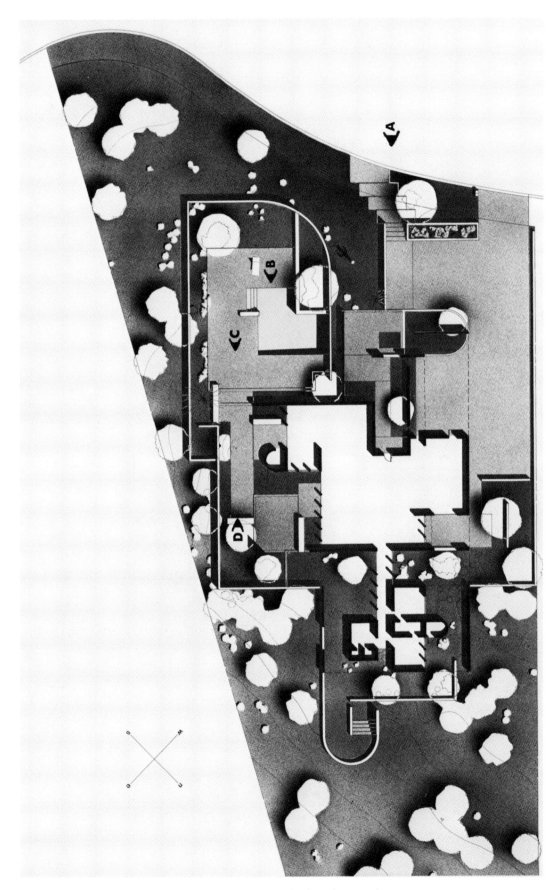

Fig. 3.36 *Plan for residence #3. See Figures 3.37 to 3.40 for four photographic views. Design by Steve Martino and Associates.*

Fig. 3.37 *View A of Residence #3. This is the front entrance to the home.*

Fig. 3.38 *View B of Residence #3, the swimming pool area.*

Fig. 3.39 *View C of Residence #3. Steps leaving the swimming pool area.*

Fig. 3.40 *View D of Residence #3, looking toward the swimming pool area.*

Materials

4

To effectively design any fabricated items you want on the site — paving, walls, steps, benches — you must have some familiarity with the materials used in such construction. You must know and consider the advantages and disadvantages of the materials you will be working with; the cost involved, availability of the materials, the strengths and sizes of the substances, and tools and equipment needed. Without this knowledge you could waste countless hours and money and never achieve the integrated, well-designed look you are after.

This chapter briefly introduces you to varieties of asphalt, concrete, brick, stone, metal, paint, plastic, and wood, including the uses for these materials. Chapter 5 illustrates specific uses in design settings, and Chapter 7 provides some discussion of the techniques and factors involved in constructing and building the landscape.

WOOD

Wood has been used as a fuel and for building materials and tools since very early in recorded history. Today it is a material with great appeal as evidenced by the amount that is used in our living environment. This appeal has carried over into the use of other materials such as plastics, where imitation wood-grain patterns provide the effect of wood at a lower cost.

In landscaping wood finds frequent use for fencing, benches and furniture, planters, decks, gazebos, paving, and so forth.

In comparison to many other materials, wood is soft, so it can easily be cut, nailed, carved and shaped. Because of its internal characteristics and voids between the cells, wood does not readily conduct heat and thus acts as an insulator. This is one reason for its warmth during skin contact. When left untreated and exposed to the weather, wood surfaces gradually bleach and become light to dark gray, and if exposed to continuous cycles of wetting and drying, the surface will begin to crack and deteriorate. Because of its porosity, wood readily accepts paints, stains, and preservatives which help to extend the life of the material. When used in structures, wood beams are more resistant to failure during a fire than steel beams — steel readily bends and warps when heated, whereas a wood beam has to burn nearly through before it fails. Several tables are provided in Chapter 7 to help you select the right size of wood beams, posts, and joists without doing extensive mathematical computations for modules of elasticity, maximum fiber in bending, maximum allowable compression, and maximum tension.

Physical Properties

Wood is made up of cellulose cells bound together by a natural cement called lignin. The cells

Fig. 4.1 *Wood decking.*

Fig. 4.2 *Split face granite pavers.*

Fig. 4.3 *Pre-cast concrete pavers.*

Fig. 4.4 *Fishscale stamped concrete.*

— called fibers in hardwoods and tracheids in softwoods — vary in size and shape according to their function. They are about 1/25 to 1/3 inch long and approximately one hundredth of their length wide. Native trees are hardwoods and softwoods. Actually these terms have nothing to do with the hardness or softness of the wood itself; in fact, some species of softwoods are harder than some species of hardwood. Hardwoods are those trees with broad leaves, and the softwoods are conifers with needle-like like or scale-like leaves. Most hardwoods shed their leaves at the end of each growing season (deciduous); the softwoods are evergreens, except for Cypress and Larch. Much of the lumber used in the construction industry is softwood because it is structurally superior and easier to handle than hardwood. Southern Pine and Douglas Fir are two currently popular species though Redwood is quite popular in the West.

Wood Products

· Lumber is sold either by lineal feet or board feet. The standard unit of measurement used by the lumber industry is the board foot, but for buyer's convenience many lumber yards will sell on the basis of lineal feet or by the piece, and their prices have been converted accordingly. Lumber is sold in 1-foot increments, ranging from 8 to 18 feet, although other lengths are available on special order at extra cost. Thicknesses begin at 1 inch for most structural lumber and then are in 2-inch increments up to 12 inches. One board foot consists of 1 inch x 12 inches x 12 inches or a square foot 1 inch thick. Any timber or board can easily be converted to board feet by multiplying the thickness in inches by the width in feet by the length in feet. For example, to determine the number of board feet in an 8-foot length of 2 x 4, multiply 2 x 0.33 x 8 = 5.333 board feet.

When we refer to a 2 x 4 x 8 we are referring to the thickness and width in nominal dimensions. The dressed (finished) or actual dimensions are less. When lumber is cut from the tree it is at actual dimension, but drying and planing smooth reduce the size to the dressed dimension which for 2 x 4 is 1-1/2 x 3-1/2. One inch thick lumber has a true

41

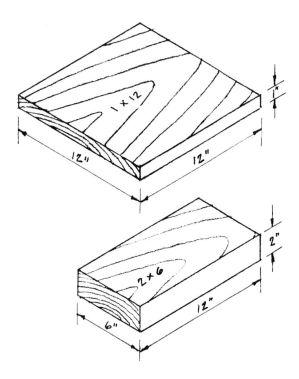

Fig. 4.5 *Measurements for board feet. Dimensions shown are nominal.*

dimension of 1/4 inch less; that is 3/4 inch thick. Boards 2 to 6 inches are dressed 1/2 inch less. Timbers above 6 inches are dressed 3/4 inch less.

When preparing or reading drawings you must remember the actual dimensions and use them. When labeling drawings it is standard practice to use the nominal dimension rather than the actual dimension. This can be confusing until you have worked with it a while and get used to the technique and practice.

Lumber is sold in several grades like utility, construction, etc. The cheaper grades are full of knots and other flaws which make their use in the landscape rather difficult. Redwood and cedar will hold up best if you purchase 'clear heart' which means the lumber will be free of the light-colored sap wood which is much more subject to decay. Pine or fir should be straight or warp free and the knots intact. All lumber should be kiln dried to reduce future warping and shrinkage.

Wood shingles are sold by the square. A square is equal to 100 square feet. Four bundles are required to cover one square. (Three bundles of asphalt shingles cover one square.) Sheet lumber includes insulation board, hardboard, particleboard, and plywood. Insulation board is a very light material used as sheathing on the exterior of the stud framework for homes and other small buildings. The outside surface is generally impregnated with asphalt emulsion, which gives it a black appearance.

Hardboard comes in a standard density or tempered (high density). The former is used for interior work, and tempered hardboard can be used for exterior exposures. Particleboard is wood chips or shavings and glue pressed into various densities, depending upon the intended use. Particleboard sheets are used in subflooring, as cores for hardwood veneers, and in the manufacture of furniture and cabinets. Plywood is an odd number of thin sheets of wood glued together. The grain of each layer is perpendicular to the adjacent layer. However, the grains on the outside layers or plys are parallel to each other to provide stability. This technique of alternating layers provides equalized strength and minimizes any dimensional changes. The standard size of plywood panels is 4 x 8 feet, although other sizes are available in some types or by special order. Thickness in general starts at 1/8 inch and increases in 1/8 inch increments to 1-1/8 inch. There are two kinds of plywood; softwood and hardwood. Softwood plywood is manufactured mainly from Douglas Fir, but several other species of wood are also used. Hardwood plywood contains much thinner veneers which are many times prefinished. These veneers may be any of the following hardwood species: walnut, cherry, oak, birch, maple, mahogany, or teak.

The three basic kinds of softwood plywood are interior, exterior and marine. Interior plywood uses non-water resistant adhesives and should be restricted to indoor use. The exterior plywood utilizes water-resistant adhesives and can be used in most exterior exposures. Marine plywood is designed for contact with water and is also good for many exterior uses. Some of these uses include fence panels, planters, sheathing for shelter roofs, and forms for concrete foundations and retaining walls. Plywood sheets or panels are graded on the basis of the presence or absence of defects on the face or surface plys. Grades range from A, which is best, down to D, which is poorest. An A-A grade applies to a grading of both sides of a sheet; a sheet thus graded has only extremely minor surface defects, and no knots or plugs and the faces rated A are sanded. A-A grade plywood is used for partitions, cabinets, furniture, and other high-quality finished woodwork. Another common plywood combination is A-D, where the A side is exposed and the D side is hidden. The D side contains knot holes, large splits, and other unsightly defects. C-D grades of plywood frequently are used for some flooring and roof sheathing. The grade C has smaller knot holes and splits than the D side.

Even though the exterior grades of plywood contain water-resistant adhesives, the surface of the wood gradually breaks down when exposed to weather; thus plywood requires a protective coating, such as paint, to prevent this deterioration. Some specialized types of plywood with veneers of redwood or cedar, intended for exterior exposure, are available. These plywood sheets come grooved or striated, brushed, rough sawn or embossed to create a variety of shadow patterns and textures.

Strips of lumber can be glued or laminated together to create beams, girders, or structural members of various sizes and shapes. Laminated beams are often used inside churches and auditoriums, foot bridges, and large decks. The wood used in laminations is generally from the softwood species and includes Douglas Fir, Larch, Southern Pine, and Redwood. Local lumber yards can help you determined the size and availability of laminated beams which can be ordered for you.

Wood Preservatives

Many woods do not have the inherent ability like redwood to resist decay and insect attack, thus preservatives: (1) creosote, (2) pentachlorophenol, and (3) metallic salts, of which the two most common are ammoniacal copper arsenate and chromated copper arsenate. Creosote is a popular preservative used to treat marine piling, utility poles and railroad ties. Pentachlorophenol has become more popular in recent years and is used to treat fence posts, utility poles, and timbers for pole barns and retaining walls. This particular chemical is diluted in petroleum distillates ranging from heavy solvents to very light mineral spirits. The heavy oils leave the wood very stable relative to moisture absorption and drying, thus making the wood more resistant to surface deterioration. However, the oil continuously bleeds for several years, preventing this wood from being painted or stained. But with the use of very light distillates, the wood can be painted. The metallic salts use water as a carrier. Wood treated with these chemicals has a greenish cast that dissipates with age after it is exposed to the outdoors. However, the wood will not become as dark of a silver-gray as untreated wood. In contrast, the penta-treated woods initially range from light to dark browns. When water is used as a carrier, the treated wood can readily be painted or stained. Creosote and timbers treated with metallic salts can be used in contact with sea water, but penta-treated wood cannot.

Over-the-counter preservatives are usually light petroleum distillates with approximately 5 percent solution of pentachlorophenol. Wood can be dipped, painted or sprayed with the solution for temporary protection, but for long-range use the wood has to be treated commercially in pressure tanks where the preservative can be forced into the

cells and the very interior of each timber. This guarantees long-range protection against insect and fungus attack and decay. Pentachlorophenol is toxic and should not be used where it can come in contact with the skin. It can also burn or damage any foliage which comes in contact with it. Woods treated with the metallic salts are best for deck surfaces, benches, railings, and other surfaces which a person or child may touch.

PAINT AND OTHER PROTECTIVE COATINGS

Paints and other coatings provide protection from corrosion and deterioration, and their inherent color can complement the landscape by creating harmony with other materials or can be accents. There are three basic categories of related coatings: paints, varnishes, and lacquers. Lacquers are used rarely in the landscape and so will not be discussed. Paint is a combination of pigment and a liquid called a vehicle or binder. The pigment imparts color, and hides the surface over which it is being placed, and influences such other paint characteristics as workability and stability after paint has been exposed. The binder is either a vegetable oil or a synthetic resin; the vegetable oil is thinned in an organic solvent, and the resin is usually dispersed in water. Solvent-thinned paints dry and harden

Table 4.1 Paintability of Softwoods

GROUP	DESCRIPTION	SPECIES
1	Woods on which the widest range of kinds and quality of paint may be expected to give good service.	Redwood Cypress Cedar
2	Woods requiring careful selection of a suitable primer to ensure good service.	White Pine
3	Woods requiring both considerable care when selecting a suitable primer and a careful maintenance program with high-quality paint.	Hemlock Spruce White Fir Ponderosa Pine
4	Woods requiring both very careful selection of the primer (must have a zinc-free housepaint primer) and the paint top coat.	Douglas Fir Larch Southern Yellow Pine

Courtesy of U.S. Forest Products Laboratory

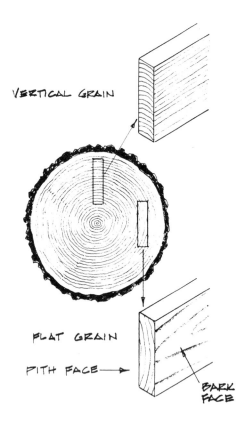

VERTICAL GRAIN

FLAT GRAIN

PITH FACE →

BARK FACE

Fig. 4.6 *Vertical grain wood holds paint better than flat grain wood.*

when their components are exposed to atmospheric oxygen. Water-thinned paints harden when their moisture evaporates from the resin particles.

Varnish differs from paint in that it consists of only the binder which is transparent. Varnish's single purpose is to provided a protective film over some kind of surface. Stains for exterior use are principally a hybrid between paint and varnish. They contain a small amount of coloring material to alter the basic color of the surface being stained, but their principal ingredients is a transparent binder or vehicle. The texture and surface characteristics of the material being covered are allowed to show through. Some heavy-bodied stains contain more pigment and come closer to approaching regular paint.

There are different formulas for paint; eight of the most common are:

1. Linseed oil-based paints were the most popular until the recent technological advances in manufacturing paint. Linseed oil is derived from flax seed.

2. Alkyd resins are made from treated vegetable oils, such as soybean, safflower, tung, or castor. The alkyd resins have largely replaced linseed oil in paint. Generally they cost less, are quite durable and flexible, and have good gloss retention. They dry by oxidation and harden fairly rapidly. They can be bought as flat or enamel and are compatible with other resins and oils.

3. Epoxy is more expensive than other ingredients but extremely tough. Generally epoxy resins are combined with other resins in many different combinations for various uses. Coal-tar epoxies withstand both fresh and salt water exposure and resist a number of chemicals.

4. Chlorinated rubber and styrene acrylate are commonly used for masonry and surfaces exposed to moisture. Chlorinated rubber is very resistant to corrosion and is quite flexible because it is 35 percent rubber.

5. Urethanes are synthetic resins, and generally, the urethanes cure faster and produce a harder, more flexible film than do alkyds. They also have better abrasion, solvent, and chemical resistance. However, urethane compounds or formulas do not hold their gloss as well as the aklyds during exterior exposure and generally cost more. Urethanes are usually superior to other varnishes as clear sealers for exterior use.

6. The most common vinyls are vinyl chloride and vinyl acetate copolymer; they have been modified to improve adhesion to metal and are commonly used in plasticized solutions for aluminum siding and galvanized cold-rolled steel.

7. Latex paints are water based and thus must be stored where they will not freeze during the winter. They must be applied when the temperature is above 40 degrees F. although some specify 50 degrees F. as a minimum.

8. Acrylics are related to latex paints. Some acrylics are used for exterior paintings, others for interiors; several are called flats, others semi-gloss. In general acrylics provide good color stability and resistance to heat, light, and weathering and impart good flexibility and strength. The principal components of acrylic latex paints are ethylacrylate and methylmethacrylate. The former is somewhat soft and has little abrasion and scrub resistance; methylmethacrylate is a hard, tough compound that when combined with ethylacrylate makes an excellent paint. Test prove that acrylic latex paints provide more trouble-free coatings over southern yellow pine because they can expand and contact in several different directions as the wood does the same.

44

Paint formulas 1 through 6 are solvent-thinned; 7 and 8 are water-thinned.

Quality

High-quality paint requires the proper blend of compatible and properly-balanced ingredients. Because of varying environmental conditions in the United States and the different kinds of surfaces to which paints are applied, you must carefully select the paint that will be most durable and most compatible with your particular situation. You will probably get your best advice by consulting local well-established stores which specialize in selling paints.

A primer is the first coat applied to a new wood surface. Its main purpose is to adhere to the surface to which it is applied and act as the adhesive for the finished coat. Primers also act as sealers when applied over porous or fibrous wood or on the paper facing of gypsum wallboard. They prevent subsequent coats from being unnecessarily soaked up by the absorbent surface. In the case of a metal a primer also acts as an anticorrosive system, thus performing an extremely important function. The finish (top) coat provide a thick or continuous film as a protection but will not adhere to the new surface by itself. Top coats also provide color and final texture and resist weather, chemicals dirt, and scrubbing.

CONCRETE

As a major construction material for steps, and walls, and paving, concrete can be formed into almost any shape, absorbs less heat than asphalt, and is readily available locally from either ready-mix plants or the ingredients can be purchased from home building and supply stores. However, concrete does reflect light, causing glare and uncomfortable light levels, so avoid large expanses of it.

Concrete is composed of four ingredients: (1) sand, (2) gravel or crushed stone, (3) water, and (4) cement. The cement binds the aggregates of sand and gravel into a permanent form. It is thus incorrect to refer to a sidewalk as a 'cement sidewalk'; the correct term is 'concrete sidewalk.'

Cement is manufactured from a combination of lime, silica, alumina, iron oxide and gypsum. The process requires considerable energy, thus its price rises with the cost of energy. A sack contains 94 pounds or 1 cubic foot of cement. Besides being used for concrete, cement is also used in making mortar for masonry work, and in mixes for grouting, parging (plastering), and stucco.

For those areas exposed to freezing and thawing, an air-entraining agent should be a part of the concrete mix. This agent is a soapy or fat-like substance which causes billions of microscopic air bubbles to form during the mixing of the concrete. It increases the concrete's resistance to moisture absorption and helps reduce deterioration of the surface from freezing and the application of salt and deicing compounds. The amount of air-entrainment should average 6 percent of the volume of the mix. The quality control you should secure air-entrained concrete from a ready-mix plant.

For small uses of concrete, such as for footings around posts, you can purchase dry-prepared mixes of concrete in sacks from lumberyards and just add water. This can be mixed in a wheelbarrow as desired. In these situations, air-entrainment is not important and money can be saved by purchasing the individual ingredients, sand, gravel and cement, and mixing your own. The sand should be fine and not exceeding 1/4 inch in size. The gravel would range from 1/4 inch up to 3/4 inch. Crushed stone provides better contact and binding with cement paste than smooth gravel. Local equipment rental companies have power mixers that can be used when you have a fair amount of concrete to mix and do not want to take the time to mix it all by hand in a wheelbarrow.

Soon after water is added to cement, an irreversible chemical reaction occurs. The setting or hardening process of concrete has begun. To attain its full strength, concrete must be cured and treated properly. Half of its strength occurs in the first 7 days, during which time it should be keep moist by sprinkling or covering with plastic. Although concrete takes almost two years to fully cure, most of its strength is developed within the first 28 days following its placement.

A good concrete mix consists of one part cement to 2-1/2 parts sand and 3-1/2 parts gravel. The amount of water to be added depends upon the moisture content of the sand and gravel. The mix should be stiff, not soupy. Too much water weakens the concrete. The correct stiffness of a mix can be measured with a slump test. This is done by taking approximately a 6-inch diameter cylinder or cone about 12 inches high and filling it with fresh concrete. When removing the cylinder the concrete should not slump more than 4 inches below the top of the adjacently placed cylinder if being used for paving or 6 inches if being poured into a retaining wall. The runnier mix for walls is needed to get the concrete around the reinforcing and fill all of the voids. A vibrator will help move the concrete into position and eliminate air pockets.

Expansion/Contraction Joints

Concrete shrinks as it cures. It also expands in warm weather. This fluctuation or movement amounts to 5/8 inch per 100 feet for each 100 degrees of temperature change. Expansion and contraction joints are needed to minimize cracking when the concrete moves. In a 5-foot wide sidewalk, an expansion joint would be placed every 30 feet and a contraction joint every 5 feet (thus creating a series of squares). More information on this will be found in Chapter 7.

Steel Reinforcing

Concrete is strengthened under compression, but weakened under tension. Compression occurs when concrete's particles are pushed together; tension occurs when a force pulls the particles apart. The tension problem can be solved by adding steel reinforcing because steel has good tensile strength. Welded wire fabric or mesh is commonly used in flat work (paving), and deformed steel bars or rods are used in walls, piers, columns and so on. Chapter 7 shows the correct position for the placement of reinforcement to obtain the greatest tensile strength. Reinforcing materials can be purchased from steel suppliers, fabricators, and most home and building supply stores.

Finishes

Concrete takes a variety of finishes. For paving the finish can be anywhere from glassy smooth to very coarse. However, a smooth surface is slick and slippery when it is wet and should be avoided for outdoor use. You can get a smooth surface by using a steel trowel. Coarse finishes can be achieved by using a wood float, a stiff broom or by exposing the aggregates through the use of chemical retardants, brushing the mix with water when it is almost set, or sandblasting the surface after it sets. More directions can be found in Chapter 7.

Many patterns can be stamped, tooled, scored, or sawed into the paving surface. Metal stamps that imitate stone, brick, or tile patterns can be stamped in the concrete surface before it completely hardened. Surface patterns can be formed by embedding wood or plastic strips into the paving surface during the finishing, or by tooling the surface with bent electrical conduit or copper wire.

Use dividers or strips of decay-resistant redwood, cedar, or cypress to form square or rectangular patterns. Uniform or random patterns of any size can be created depending upon the effect desired. The wood dividers can double as expansion and contraction joints.

You can create additional patterns by using strips of masonry units as dividers, such as bricks. Where foot traffic wear down a broom finish, the use of abrasive silicon carbide and aluminum oxide grains will provide a longer-lasting, nonslip finish.

However, silicon carbide has a sparkle, which may or may not be desirable.

Many finishing techniques can be used for concrete walls from a plain form finish to a complex pattern. A form finish is one which results naturally when the forms are removed. The quality of the finish is dependent on the forms. If they are plywood units which are relatively new and free of knots the finish will be relatively uniform if the concrete was poured continuously and vibrated to remove air pockets and inconsistencies. At any rate, there is a probability that the form joints will show as well as the form ties. (Form ties are small steel rods that hold both sides of the forms in place and help maintain a uniform thickness for the wall.) Coating the forms with oil helps to provide a smoother finish surface and makes the forms easier to remove as well. Rubbing the entire wall with a paste of cement and sand mixed, and utilizing a Carborundum stone to remove surface irregularities like form joints, can give a wall a uniform textural finish similar to the wood float finish for paving. The paste is also good for filling in the holes left by the form ties, but if the mixture is used for the holes only an unattractive patchy effect will be created. It is also almost impossible to match the color of the paste to the concrete.

Rubber mats or patterns formed with fiberglass can be inserted inside the usual forms to create any number of creative finishes with very smooth surfaces. To make corrugated or irregular rough patterns place various sizes of wood strips inside the forms. Sandblasting the wood strips before pouring the concrete against them will bring out the grain. After a wall is cured, the surface can be sandblasted or bush hammered (bush fitting on an air hammer) to create a uniform texture or expose the aggregate. These last processes are best preformed by a skilled contractor.

Another way to finish concrete walls is to cover the surface with brick, stone, or precast concrete veneer slabs of exposed aggregates. Precast concrete provides a high quality and a carefully controlled exposure of the aggregates. These techniques are much more expensive to render than conventional ones, but they can be especially attractive and useful in landscaping. For instance, the brick or stone used in the home can be repeated in a wall, visually extending the color and texture into the landscape and visually tying the house and garden together into a uniform whole.

Precast Concrete

Products in this category include standard-sized concrete masonry units (including concrete block), pavers of varying sizes and thicknesses, precast or cast stone with exposed aggregates for veneers, utility structures (catch basins, manholes, and so forth), burial vaults, and pipe. Pavers may be square, rectangular, hexagons, round, or several unusual shapes approximately the size of brick, but interlocking. They vary in thickness from 1-1/2 inch up to 3 inches and are intended to be placed by hand over a porous material such as sand which can be easily leveled and compacted. More information can be found in Chapter 7. Precast concrete has much greater quality than cast-in-place concrete because the mixing, handling, and curing conditions have been carefully controlled to ensure a superior product.

In place of gravel in pre-cast concrete cinders, expanded slag, expanded shale, clay, slate, or volcanic materials are used depending upon local conditions. Expanded shale can reduce the weight of precast units by approximately 35 percent.

Concrete masonry units are produced in many sizes, shapes and patterns, but a few widely used units in standard-sizes are available at concrete block manufacturers, or most masonry supply stores. These units (block) are commonly used for walls and partitions, as a backup for brick or stone, as masonry in planters and retaining walls, and as foundations.

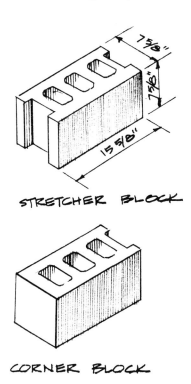

STRETCHER BLOCK

CORNER BLOCK

Fig. 4.7 *Two types of concrete block.*

There are stretcher blocks, corner blocks, and so forth, in 4, 6, and 8-inch widths, 8 inches high and 16 inches long. Actually the true dimensions are 3/8

inch less, to allow for mortar. Mortar is a mix of cement, sand, water and occasionally lime, that forms a thick paste which is placed between each layer of blocks or brick. The same paste can be used to grout the unfilled joints between block, tile, or brick.

Color

Color pigments can be mixed into concrete before the concrete is poured, or mixed into the upper surface during the finishing process. Stains and paints can be applied after the concrete has cured. Be aware that uniformity and consistency of color when using pigments and stains is difficult to achieve. Oil-based paints will likely peel or flake off, but latex masonry paints will hold up well where not exposed to foot traffic.

Only high quality mineral pigments should be mixed into concrete; impurities reduce the strength of the mix. Even pure pigment should not exceed 10 percent of the weight of the cement, or 9.4 pounds per sack, to preserve the strength of the concrete mix without weakening it.

Slight gray colors to much darker grays can be achieved by adding black iron oxide. Other colors and pigments included red-red oxide of iron, brown-brown oxide of iron, buff-yellow oxide of iron, blue-cobalt oxide, and green-chromium oxide.

MASONRY

Masonry includes brick, related clay products, and stone. Although brick and stone are not necessarily related in their characteristics, the way they are used in landscaping can be quite similar. These materials can be used for paving, steps, walls, and so forth.

Brick

In use since early recorded history, brick is manufactured from clay or shale that has been mined, pulverized, mixed, formed, cut to size, dried, and fired in a kiln for several hours or days at 1600 to 2000 degrees F. The quality of the raw materials and the length of the firing process determine durability. The inherent or added minerals determine color, which varies according to the length of time, temperature, and oxidation in the firing process.

Dark-colored bricks, which ring when hit together, generally are dense, well-fired and very durable. Salmon-colored units, which sound dull, are usually soft and prone to early deterioration when exposed to weather. The softer brick absorbs water more readily and thus is subject to considerable stress in freeze-thaw cycles. High quality bricks have little, if any, absorption characteristics, so they are not as susceptible to freeze-thaw damage. Bricks that absorb water too rapidly rob the mortar of the moisture needed to ensure the complete chemistry of set and arrival at full strength. Bricks are available in many shapes, colors, sizes, and glazes. Standard building brick used for walls are 2-1/4 inches thick by 3-3/4 inches wide by 7-3/4 inches long. Check with your local masonry supplier for other sizes. Brick pavers are generally solid units; building bricks contain various number of holes or cores in their centers (which helps to bond each brick to the next

CORED BRICK

Fig. 4.8 *Standard brick with cores.*

layer above or below). Bricks vary enough from batch to batch in the manufacturing process so that matching is difficult if continuity of color is required. Thus you should order the total quantity of bricks needed to complete a project from the same batch. Remember that not all sizes, shapes, colors, and textures are available in any one locality. Some suppliers ship regularly to various parts of the country, but shipping cost is a major consideration when you decide to use brick.

Clay Units

Clay patio tile and quarry tile come in several different forms. Quarry tile is generally square, thin, and quite hard. Because it is thin, it is usually placed over a concrete base and mortared in place. Clay patio tiles are soft and available in many shapes; they are best where freeze-thaw cycles are not a problem. Clay tiles are also useful if you are building free-standing walls. Ceramic or glazed tiles are highly colorful; mosaic patterns can be created by using an assortment of the tiles. Outdoors they are sometimes used in pools and fountains or on building walls. The most common sizes are 1 to 4 inch squares; other sizes are also available. The tiles are quite thin and thus are always used as a veneer over a solid surface material.

Stone

Stone is an old as the earth and available in infinite sizes, shapes, colors, and textures. It is an excellent asset in landscaping where a natural character and richness is desired. The local availability of certain types of stone and the cost of transporting stones are limiting factors in using them.

The six most common kinds of stone are:

1. Sedimentary stones, such as sandstone, brownstone, bluestone, and limestone, are somewhat 'soft' and thus easy to cut and work, but they are subject to staining and weathering because of their porosity. They can be used for paving, steps, walls, and so forth.

2. Marble, a metamorphic form of limestone, is harder, and more durable (10,500 psi) than sedimentary stone, easy to carve and polish, and popular because of its patterns and beauty. It is commonly used for statuary and as a veneer for paving, steps, and walls.

3. Slate, a metamorphic form of shale, is a hard and durable stone that varies from blue to gray to black, with some red types. It is cut thin like quarry tile and mortared in place over a concrete base for use as paving, or even thinner pieces can be used as shingles.

4. Granite, an igneous rock, is quite hard and thus very durable (26,000 to 30,000 psi). It ranges from an almost white to dark gray with some pink forms. It can be carved and cut into many shapes and sizes and resists staining and weathers well. Where it occurs naturally, granite is frequently used for road curbs and paving cobblestones. It is widely used in cut sheets or panels as a veneer for walls, steps, pavers, and for statuary.

5. Volcanic rock is dark and limited in use to lump sizes. It is not practical to carve, cut, and use like the other types of stone, and it is coarse, sharp, and harsh to bare skin. It can be used for rubble-type retaining walls and for rock gardens.

6. Traprock is fine-grained, hard stone that fractures easily. It is more useful as an aggregate for concrete and as a base course for paving, and in mulches.

Three types of finishes are generally available for most stone. The one with the coarsest texture and an irregular surface is called split-face. A sawn-face is level in appearance but feels like a sandy surface to the touch. When polished to a glass-like surface the stone has been buffed by a Carborundum wheel. Letters and patterns can be incised into the surface of the stone by chiseling or sandblasting. Check your local masonry or stone suppliers for samples and availability.

Glass

Glass building blocks are regularly 3 7/8 inches thick and come in squares measuring 6, 8, and 12 inches and in rectangles measuring 4 x 8 inches and 6 x 8 inches. Blocks are assembled much like other masonry products using mortar joints. Blocks are typically hollow in the center, have some sound insulating capabilities, and transmit light. With their thickness, most blocks offer complete visual privacy enabling their use as walls or visual screens while allowing light to pass through. With lights installed columns of night light can be used for special effects either alone or installed in fountains and swimming pools. Bollards and benches are other uses.

METALS

Iron and Steel

Many times these words are used interchangeably, but iron is less refined than steel. The latter is iron with other materials added to make it a better product. In the landscape iron is used to make wrought iron fences. It is also used to make pipe. Steel is used to make nails, bolts, screws, and many kinds of fasteners. Structural steel consists of angles, tees, tubing, pipes and 'I' beams. Steel subjected to the weather will rust. Thus it must be coated with a rust-resistant material. Sheet steel, nails and pipe are typically cleaned with acid and then dipped into a bath of melted zinc, a process called 'hot dip galvanizing.' Bolts and screws are electroplated with cadmium to prevent rust. This turns the steel from a dark gray to a bright silvery appearance almost as bright as polished chrome.

Aluminum

This silvery-white metal is popular because it is lightweight and rustproof. Alloys are usually created to give aluminum strength. It is used in the landscape in the form of nails, handrails, light fixtures, fasteners, and so forth. Where the natural color of the metal does not harmonize, colors are anodized to its surface.

Copper

Copper is rustproof and very resistant to corrosion. When it is exposed to damp air, copper's surface changes from a bright reddish orange to a dark reddish brown, and after long exposure it becomes coated with a green film called patina, which in turn protects the copper from further corrosion. It is a good conductor of electricity and thus is used for electrical wiring. It can also be used in sheet form as flashing and roofing, though it is much more expensive than aluminum or galvanized sheet steel.

Bronze and Brass

Bronze and brass are two alloys of copper that are rather widely used. Bronze is an alloy of copper and tin, with the amount of tin varying from a small amount to 25 percent. Occasionally other metals are used for special purposes; in particular phosphorus hardens and strengthens bronze. Like copper, bronze resists corrosion and has an indefinite life span. Bronze is used in sculpture, statuary, bells, hardware, light fixtures, ornaments, and plumbing valves.

Brass is a mixture of copper and zinc. The amount of copper in this alloy varies from 55 to more than 95 percent. The color of brass varies with the composition of the ingredients; when it contains approximately 70 percent copper, the alloy is a clear golden yellow metal sometimes called 'yellow brass.' When 80 percent or more copper is used, it begins to turn red and is called 'red brass.' With the higher zinc content the brass has its strongest and toughest quality. At 55 percent copper the alloy can become rather hard and brittle. Brass is widely used in the manufacture of hardware, electrical and plumbing fixtures, and metal decorations.

PLASTICS

Plastics are synthetic chemical compounds derived from such sources as coal and petroleum, with some limestone, salt, and water also used. Hundreds of different plastic formulas and characteristics have been developed. Some plastics are soft and pliable, whereas others are hard; there are both opaque and transparent plastics. The price of plastics is affected by the rising cost of petroleum and other energy sources, as are most other materials because energy is used in their production and processing.

Following is a brief tabulation of several kinds of plastics and their uses as they apply to landscaping.

1. Vinyl is used for waterstops for pool and retaining wall expansion joints to prevent leaking, membrane waterproofing, and color coating for chainlink fences.

Fig. 4.9 *Corrugated drainage pipe.*

49

Fig. 4.10 *Urethane (dark strip near bottom of photo) cover the expansion joint in paving.*

2. Polyethylene is available as sheet plastic for waterproofing, flexible pipe for irrigation systems, corrugated pipe for drainage, and insulation for electrical wire.

3. Urethane is a flexible sealant applied to the upper surface of expansion joints.

4. Epoxy is applied like paint to seal the insides of pools and fountains. It is also used as glues and, when combined with fiberglass cloth, can be a reinforced plastic for planters, benches, waste containers, and other street furniture items.

5. Phenolics are very hard, durable plastics that, when laminated in thin sheets, can be used as veneers for doors, tabletops, and so on. Wood grain and marble patterns can be effectively simulated in these materials.

6. Acrylics are used as lenses for light fixtures.

7. Nylon is used in gears, tees and ells in plastic plumbing systems; and as bristles for brooms and paint brushes.

8. Polyvinylchloride (PVC) is used as piping for irrigation systems. It is rigid in contrast to polyethylene pipe.

9. Polystyrene is widely used for foam insulation panels. When used along the sides of planters, it both insulates the soil from the cold and acts as an expansion cushion when the soil freezes.

10. Polypropylene is utilized for pipe and fittings, wire insulation and rope.

Fig. 4.11 *Epoxy and fiberglass are used to make the table top. Umbrella top and seat material are vinyl. Steel legs are coated with white plastic.*

Fig. 4.12 *Light lenses are white acrylic.*

ASPHALT

Asphalt, a product derived from petroleum or coal-tar, ranges in color from dark brown to black. It is available in a variety of grades and types, but for landscaping a basic semisolid form known as asphalt cement is generally used. The advantages of asphalt are that it is waterproof adhesive, it is durable; resistant to acids, alkalis, and salts, and when mixed with mineral aggregates, forms a controllable plastic substance. Unfortunately, asphalt absorbs the sun's heat, making it painful to bare feet. Also asphalt dissolves if gasoline or other flammable liquids are spilled on it.

Asphalt Concrete Pavement

About 90 percent of the roads and parking lots in the United States are made of asphalt concrete pavement. It is also used for curbs, tennis and basketball courts, tracks, bicycle and golf-cart paths, and sidewalks--any areas that get wet and tear and weight. Asphalt concrete curbs can be constructed by a machine that extrudes (pushes out) the hot mix on to the top of the edge of asphalt paving. Although less expensive than poured-in-place concrete, asphalt curbs are easily damaged by tires and snowplows. Asphalt is a product that must be handled by those contractors who have the specialized knowledge and equipment, and is not something you can do yourself, except to apply the asphalt emulsion sealer after the asphalt pavement is in place. Because asphalt is a petroleum based product its costs are continually increasing, but it still may be less expensive than to hire a contractor to place concrete, such as for a driveway. If you have the skill or desire to pour your own concrete, you may be able to save money over having a contractor place asphalt pavement. Doing a cost estimate for both before you proceed, keeping in mind the advantages and disadvantages of each type of pavement, will help you make the best decision.

Asphaltic concrete pavement (also called 'blacktop') is a paving mix of various amounts of asphalt cement, coarse and fine aggregates, mineral filler and dust. The aggregates are crushed stone, slag, or gravel with angular, pitted, or rough surface textures. Polished aggregates should not be used because they do not bind together well. All aggregates must be free from clay, silt, and organic matter such as grass, leaves, twigs, and so forth. The wearing course, applied above the base, contains finer aggregates, which supply density and tightness. The wearing course thus provides a smoother surface and resists water penetration. An additional leveling course of asphalt cement and fine aggregate can be applied if a precision slope is necessary such as on a tennis court.

A 3- to 4-inch base of asphalt pavement can be laid over 4 to 6 inches of compacted gravel. The pavement should then be covered with 1-1/2 to 2 inches of finer material (coarse sand and pea gravel), to make a smooth top surface. Several months later the asphalt pavement can be sealed with an asphalt emulsion to restore the black color (the emulsion is rolled on like paint). Full-depth asphaltic concrete (5 to 12 inches) is recommended for driveways. The depth depends on the weight of vehicles that will be using the driveway, the soil and freeze-thaw conditions. Consult a reputable local asphalt pavement supplier (preferably one with a soils engineer on its staff) for recommendations concerning your particular situation. Full-depth asphalt concrete can be laid directly on a subgrade, without gravel, as long as the soil is free of debris and has been thoroughly compacted, otherwise the pavement will settle and crack. Surface drainage for asphalt pavement should never be less than 1 percent or 1-foot drop for every 100 feet. A 2 percent or 1/4 inch/foot slope is considered ideal.

On well-drained soils, thinner applications of asphalt concrete paving can be used for sidewalks than those suggested above for driveways. Where a high quality finished appearance is desired, or the design lines need to be well-established, the use of steel or treated wood edging is recommended.

Color coatings are available for asphalt for applications in the form of strips or solid patterns for game areas, or wherever you might want to alter the black appearance of asphalt concrete pavement. These coatings need to be applied by trained personnel and you will need to contract this with your asphalt concrete supplier. Let newly laid asphalt pavement set 30 days before applying a sealer or a color coating.

Construction Design

5

The purpose of this chapter is to introduce you to landscape features, other than plants, such as paving, edgings, steps, walls, fences, decks, shelters, benches, planters and fountains. Design variety is almost infinite depending upon one's imagination, so in this chapter you will see only a small potential for the variety of design that is possible. Many of these designs have been created by landscape architects whose knowledge, experience, and training in the use of materials makes it possible for them to create a greater variety of design than the homeowner whose knowledge and experience may be quite limited. The more one becomes acquainted with materials and gains skill in working with them, the more variety he can create in the use and placement of those materials. Chapter 4 describes materials and how they relate to each other, and Chapter 7 will describe and illustrate ways of building at least some of the ideas you see illustrated in this chapter.

Where space permits, and privacy is desired, a subtle entrance to a home can be designed and planned. The driveway and placement of the plant materials can be designed to meander, hiding the home from view and creating a dramatic effect for the visitor. The design style that characterizes such an entrance would be curvilinear.

A central parking area for a group of homes may be broken up with islands where existing trees can be preserved, or new trees planted (see Figure 5.3).

On most small sites the home is located close to the road. Parking can be adjacent to the road as shown in Figure 5.4. The parking ends where the brick begins, and the entrance to the home is to the left, hidden from view of the parking lot by the partial wood screen. Visitors to the home can walk from the parking to the front door under the sheltered canopy to protect them from rain and sun. All of the design here is modular (all lines are at right angles to each other).

When the site drops away from the access road and parking, a deck can be used to connect the parking to the front entrance of the home. This is illustrated in Figure 5.5, where on the left, the deck has been built around some existing trees to allow them to remain. The design style used here is completely modular.

A variation can be created from the modular design approach to an entrance by introducing curves which can be very dramatic. Figure 5.6 shows how exposed aggregate is used for the paving rather than plain concrete to provide a pleasing texture and soften the glare of rectangles of varying sizes is also used to break up the monotony which can be a problem in modular patterns.

With modular design, it is easy to change from just a straight entrance to one which allows additions such as a sitting area as shown in Figure 5.7. A low wall and planters add three-dimensional interest and make the entrance much more inviting.

Fig. 5.1 *An entry drive of exposed aggregate concrete with paver brick inserts. Design by Mark M. Holeman Inc.*

Fig. 5.2 *A driveway court and entry to the front of the home. The pavement is ceramic tile in two shades of gray. Design by Mark M. Holeman Inc.*

Fig. 5.3 *Parking for a group of homes. Design by Theodore Brickman Co.*

Fig. 5.4 *Canopied entrance from parking. Design by LaPorte County Landscaping.*

Fig. 5.5 *Deck entrance from parking. Design by Blair and Zalk.*

Fig. 5.6 *Courtyard entrance to home. Design by Theodore Brickman Co.*

Fig. 5.8 *Entrance with modular patterns. Design by Doede, Inc.*

Fig. 5.7 *Modular style front entry using tile and concrete.*

Fig. 5.9 *Entrance with stone paving and walls. Design by Browning Day Mullins Dierdorf, Inc.*

Fig. 5.10 *Side yard depressed to serve as a storm retention basin. A xeriscape with native plants, rock, stone mulch and drip irrigation.*

Fig. 5.11 *Mounding in a side yard. Design by LaPorte County Landscaping.*

Pre-cast concrete pavers can be used in place of cast-in-place concrete to create a modular pattern with unlimited design possibilities. Random patterns of many types can be created according to your imagination. This type of paver allows you to experiment by moving the pavers around on the existing surface before final installation in order to see what kind of pattern appeals to you most. One such pattern is shown in Figure 5.8. This again is a modular design. These pavers can be easily installed by anyone, though you should keep in mind that the grass or ground covers will grow between them and will need to be trimmed.

Gravel can be used for a driveway, but it is messy and hard to control unless an edging and stabilizer are used. Some of the gravel will travel into adjacent grass and planting beds, and some smaller pieces will cling to shoes and end up in the house. Gravel does offer a paving surface that is better than just plain dirt. The cost is less than asphalt or concrete and gravel will provide an adequate surface until you can afford to install a more expensive, durable and less troublesome paving surface.

Walks, paths, and drives constructed of decomposed granite, crushed limestone or other natural materials containing a small aggregate with fines or soil can be stabilized. This will reduce erosion and the messiness of loose materials. One such stabilizer is organic in composition and non-toxic to human, animal, and plant contact. The top three to four inches of decomposed granite is tilled and one pound of stabilizer per 10 square feet thoroughly mixed in to the same depth. The surface is smoothed and water applied to the full depth. After the water dissipates and while still moist, the surface is rolled smooth and compacted. When the surface is completely dry, it can be used. See Appendix B for the source of this stabilizer.

Natural materials such as stone paving, stone walls, and hand-split shingles can soften the harsh lines that are sometimes created in modular design. Such a design approach is more expensive, but offers a warmth and richness to the front entrance that you may find very appealing (see Figure 5.9).

Mounding can be used in combination with curvilinear design to create greater visual appeal in the landscape. Such mounding can be subtlety placed in the front or along the side yard (if there is room) such as in Figure 5.11. Sometimes this mounding is also referred to as 'earth sculpture' or 'land sculpture.' When done well it is an art form and adds much to the aesthetics of the residential landscape.

There are other ways of handling a side yard where there is a large roof overhand. Openings can be made in the overhang to provide more light and rain for the plantings below. Vines can be trained to grow up the wall and cover a portion of the overhand for greater interest as shown in Figure 5.12. Side yards can also be used for screened-in storage areas, potting benches, herb gardens, etc. Because space is usually quite tight between side yards, modular design is the best approach to solving the use of the small space.

A modular material can be used tolerate a curvilinear path. Precast pavers laid on sand can be made to follow a curved line, as shown in Figure 5.13.

Round precast concrete pavers in varying diameters lend themselves to a good design harmony with a curvilinear designed path as in Figure 5.14. The edges, however, are a little more irregular than those shown in Figure 5.13.

Fig. 5.12 *Attractive side yard. Design by Theodore Brickman Co.*

Fig. 5.13 *Curvilinear path using rectangular pre-cast pavers.*

Fig. 5.14 *Curvilinear path using round pre-cast concrete pavers.*

Fig. 5.16 *Rock and stone steps create harmony. Design by A. E. Bye and Associates.*

Where rock occurs naturally the use of the same stone and exposed aggregate concrete together create a design harmony. The use of irregular or curvilinear lines is also compatible with the design style (see Figure 5.15).

The use of stone for steps provides a much better design harmony than would concrete, brick or wood, when large boulders of stone are used to retain the slope (see Figure 5.16).

When a house is long and linear, the steps can harmonize with the same bold linear lines and provide a dramatic technique for changing levels and create a sense of openness and spaciousness as shown in Figure 5.17.

Fig. 5.17 *Broad steps create a sense of openness. Design by A. E. Bye and Associates.*

Fig. 5.15 *There is harmony in using rock with exposed aggregate concrete.*

Dining and sitting areas adjacent to a home can take several design characteristics, shapes and forms, depending upon the circumstances and the materials that are used. Figure 5.18 features the use of bluestone and a low wall for enclosure. The materials are modular and the design pattern for the entire patio area is modular in character. Figure 5.19 utilizes concrete with an exposed aggregate and a modular pattern created with the dividing lines in the pavement. The bench and table are wood as well as the enclosing fence which provides privacy for the family as they dine. The sitting area in Figure 5.20 uses pre-cast concrete pavers. Figure 5.21 is modular design in character but the paving pattern is fish-scale using cut brick, and, thus, the modular pattern is somewhat modified in a more interesting way. The paving has been placed around an existing oak tree.

Fig. 5.18 *Bluestone dining area. Design by Claire Bennett.*

Fig. 5.20 *Sitting area with pre-cast concrete pavers adjacent to a swimming pool. Landscape design by Barbara J. Ziolkowski.*

Fig. 5.19 *Exposed aggregate patio. Design by Doede, Inc.*

Fig. 5.21 *Dining area with fishscale paving pattern.*

Fig. 5.22 *Bluestone and brick modular patio. Design by Browning Day Mullins Dierdorf, Inc.*

When woods and ravines surround a home, the little remaining space left behind the home can be devoted entirely to a patio for dining, family entertaining and activities as shown in Figure 5.22. To the far right a dining table is close to the kitchen and the dining room inside the house. For dining further away from the house, the barbecue pit shown at the left, is provided for cooking and other tables and chairs are located elsewhere on the patio. The design is modular and the landscape architect used bluestone and brick. Limestone was used for the walls creating partial enclosure.

When space is tight walls can provide immediate enclosure and privacy for a small living space. Using wood dividers in the paving design (see Figure 5.23).

Fig. 5.23 *Small enclosed living space.*

Fig. 5.24 *Sitting area adjacent to a pool with ceramic tile in two shades of gray to match the gray Indiana limestone veneer used on the house. The trees in the background are natives which line the edge of a reservoir. Design by Mark M. Holeman Inc.*

If you do not like to look out of a basement room into nothing but window wells, the soil can be lowered adjacent to the basement, thus creating an outdoor room at a different level such as shown in Figure 5.25. This provides more light and better views to the basement rooms. It will add to the value of your property as well as making living much more comfortable and interesting. Before creating such a room you will need to be sure you can drain such a sunken area. The design style of the area shown is curvilinear, but could just as well be modular if you so choose.

The modular design can be made more intriguing by using a variety of materials for the paving surfaces. Further appeal can be achieved by changing elevations either by terracing or by the use of a deck if the site is flat. Introducing a small pool or fountain adds further charm and can become a focal point. Such is the case for Figure 5.26 where wood, brick and grass contrast with each other as paving surfaces. The pool is close enough to be viewed from the deck or the outdoor dining table. Planting around the periphery provides complete privacy from adjacent neighbors. Note the way that modular design is being used: rectangles interplay with each other in a random pattern that is not monotonous.

A small site does not have to include grass in the design. Neither does a modular design have to include all squares, but a combination of squares and rectangles can work together to make a pleasing

Fig. 5.25 *Sunken area for a brighter basement. Design by Theodore Brickman Co.*

Fig. 5.27 *Modular design with changes of level and texture. Design by Theodore Brickman Co.*

Fig. 5.26 *Modular deck and patio. Design by Theodore Brickman Co.*

60

design. While rock is not a modular design material, it can be used to introduce an aspect of nature to modular design and provide some visual relief and variety to the modules as shown in Figure 5.27.

While in some cases the design can create a definite separation between the patio and the rest of the garden, it is possible to cause one to lead into the other by the way the whole design is created. Note in Figure 5.28 that the paving rectangles lead from the patio out into the grass, and there is not strong design line that separates the two as illustrated in some of the other gardens in this chapter.

Circles can be used in a modular design pattern if they are handled carefully; they can also add relief to the straight lines of the modular design and create additional aesthetic interest as in Figure 5.29.

How do you handle a site where the finish grade drops too rapidly away from the house and yet still provide a fair amount of outdoor living space? The modular design in Figure 5.30 shows one way to solve the problem. When a deck is more than about 12 inches off the ground it is desirable to have a safety railing which can be easily designed to both guard the edge of the platform and still be aesthetically pleasing. Leaving an existing tree in the patio area will add beauty, variety and shade.

Fig. 5.28 *Use of rectangles in modular design. Design by Theodore Brickman Co.*

Fig. 5.29 *A patio area using brick pavers. Design by Mark M. Holeman Inc.*

Fig. 5.30 *Modular deck with existing trees. Design by Royston, Hanamoto and Mayes.*

Even though wood is a modular material, angles can be created from it and it can be used to add considerable interest to what might otherwise be a drab situation. In Figure 5.31 the property slopes from the left to the right and thus considerably more steps are used on the right side of the deck than on the left. Note also how the functions and features of the safety rail and bench are combined.

A deck with benches, a fire pit, and shrub beds, with the whole area enclosed by a fence, can be used for the design of a small site as shown in the modular design used in Figure 5.32. Note that while the deck is modular, it is not square, and while the central portion is spacious the narrow extensions on either side add linearity and esthetic interest. The fire pit area is separated somewhat from the main part of the patio by recessing it and then enclosing it with benches backed up by planting.

When there is a dramatic view available from the house to the countryside beyond or perhaps a lake, as in Figure 5.33, the design of the landscape should not detract from such a view. Note that the edge of the deck is protected and identified by a bench which also serves as a railing. Because it is low it does not interfere with the line of sight from within the house. The wood surface of the deck has been designed in a checkerboard pattern which creates a more interesting surface for a large deck.

Fig. 5.31 *Angular style deck designed by Doede Inc.*

Fig. 5.33 *Checkerboard deck designed by Larry Halprin.*

Fig. 5.32 *Modular deck and fire pit. Design by Alex Pierce.*

Fig. 5.34 *Oriental style garden. Design by LaPorte County Landscaping.*

An exotic oriental effect, as seen in Figure 5.34, can be created by removing some of the soil in the backyard in a meandering pattern, filling the depression with gravel, and adding some treated timbers for stepping stones. Much of the design here is curvilinear, but the deck is modular. The viewer is not too aware of the shape of the deck because of the many meandering lines including the open (snow fence) shelter above and surrounding it.

Modular design can be given variety by the introduction of changes in level and in shape as shown in Figure 5.35. The coarseness of the exposed aggregate further softens the harshness of the straight lines.

Water in motion adds considerable pleasure to any landscape design as well as mask unwanted sounds like industries or roads which may be near the home site (see Figure 5.36).

Fig. 5.35 *Multi-level modular design by John Douglas.*

Fig. 5.36 *The sight and sound of water enhances a living space.*

Modular designed fountains can be used to advantage where the design of the rest of the site is the same style, but in more open, larger settings where nature can be allowed to dominate, natural ponds or bodies of water can be utilized such as in Figure 5.37. However, if water does not occur naturally, then ponds can be created by careful excavation in the site. Usually these man-made ponds reflect curving lines such as in Figure 7.38. If ponds are not established in a natural water table, they may need something like a plastic liner to help them retain the water. They may also need a well or other water source to maintain the water level and offset the effects of evaporation. Ponds on flat sites are much more interesting when some of the excavated soil is used to create a few mounds along the edges as shown in Figure 5.39. The design style is curvilinear both horizontally as well as vertically.

Fig. 5.38 *Man-made pond with a natural appearance. Design by Theodore Brickman Co.*

Fig. 5.39 *Man-made pond with mounding. Design by Walker Harris Associates, Inc.*

Fig. 5.37 *Natural pond as a setting for a house.*

Fig. 5.40 *A pond in an oriental style garden.*

A piece of sculpture can be used as a dramatic focal point in a landscape composition. It may also double as a piece of play sculpture as illustrated in Figure 5.41. Sand around the base helps protect children from injury as they climb up, over, and under the sculpture and enjoy it as a piece of play equipment. The design style is curvilinear.

Wood can be used to create a sculptural focal point in a garden. Six inch by six inch timbers cut at angles and installed in an irregular pattern were used o create the ten foot tall piece of wood sculpture shown in Figure 5.42, which is a combination of modular and angular design styles. There is harmony because in the sculpture the angles are all the same even though in various positions. The uniform modules of 6x6 timbers also add to the harmony of the design.

Fig. 5.41 *Backyard play sculpture.*

Fig. 5.42 *Wood sculpture (10 feet tall) as a focal point in a garden with the background of a forest.*

Night lighting introduces a completely new dimension in design, but it is difficult to describe it as any particular design style. Light forms round patterns from its source, so it may be considered curvilinear, but the shadows are certainly not since they create angular lines, or very chaotic patterns from shrub and tree branches. Lighting is furthermore three dimensional because space to the side and above can be dark, and thus create the feeling of space and make the space that is light take on the appearance of a room.

Lighting extends nighttime space — making outdoor space usable for an extended number of hours. It helps diminish the problems of safety and security, and when carefully designed will add to the esthetic values of the home and site. It can also create focal points and make winter that season a more pleasant experience (see Figures 5.43 to Figure 5.46).

Fig. 5.46 *Lighting for winter effects.*

Fig. 5.43 *Patio lighting.*

66

Fig. 5.44 *Patio and play area lighting.*

Fig. 5.45 *Step and path lighting.*

Planting Design

6

After you analyze the site, consider the functional needs that are to take place on site, and plan the design of constructed items, you are ready to consider the remaining element in the overall design: the plants. This is an important step because a landscape design becomes a work of art only when all the elements are properly arranged in an aesthetic composition that is pleasing to the eye.

Most planting designs are influenced by the characteristics of the site and the architectural elements of the house. You must closely coordinate your use of plant line, form, texture, color, scale, proportion, repetition, unity and emphasis with the same characteristics or elements used in the architecture of the house and other structures, such as walls, fences, paving, pools, planters, benches, and so on. The 'constructed' parts of the design are an integral part of it, necessary to impart three-dimensional relief to the landscape, and they cannot be separated from the aesthetic and functional considerations given to plants. The various elements must come together to form a harmonious whole, in much the same way as the various notes in a successful musical composition blend to form pleasant sounds. Besides the design elements, you

also have to consider the functional characteristics of plants: the need for visual and physical barriers, climate control, erosion control, and so forth. Our detailed discussion of these traits — covered later in the chapter — will help you intelligently plan your landscape design.

The design of a carefully planned landscape has unique qualities that distinguish it from other works of art. Whereas a painting is created on the flat surface of a canvas and a piece of sculpture is displayed on a pedestal, the designed landscape is intended to be walked through, around, over, and under. In most arts viewers have to focus their senses on an effect that has been produced in a condensed or restricted space. But in a landscape design the artistic effect can be experienced in many diverse ways because viewers are actually within the design. In a properly designed landscape, scale can be measured in relation to the size of the people and the size of the space they need for their activities.

Futhermore, the landscape composition changes as people move through it and vistas emerge and disappear; it is also constantly modified by ever-changing shadows as the sun crosses the sky, and the clouds move, not to mention the change created

in plants by the spring, the appearance and aroma of flowers and fruit in summer, the color transformation in the fall, and the bareness of the branches in the winter. In your planning efforts you will face tremendous challenges to create a work of art that is aesthetically pleasing to all the senses, as well as functional and harmonious with the physical environment in which it must survive.

Here we define and describe a number of terms that comprise the elements of designing with plants. Plants, in and of themselves, possess form, texture, and color. These characteristics may be used in a landscape composition to create line, mass, variety, repetition, balance, and emphasis. You must consider the ultimate size or mature growth of a plant in scale with the space that it must occupy, next to people, objects, and buildings. If a plant is too small, it will seem lost; if it is too large, it will crowd its space or look overpowering. Remember that the placement of plants in a landscape design creates or defines space. Finally, you should also take into account growth characteristics — some plants, like morning glories, can ultimately strangle other plants, and the growth habits of some plants may create a growth that is too dense.

AESTHETICS OF LANDSCAPE DESIGN

Plants, as one of the most visible manifestations of nature, have always fascinated human beings. As spring emerges each year, we stop to admire the growing wild flowers and the new leaves on trees and shrubs. In the house garden, you can discover the crocus appearing and coming into bloom, followed by yellow forsythia and then a multitude of other blossoms in subsequent weeks. This fascination with plant color may wane somewhat in the heat of the summer, but as the leaves are infused with the fiery colors of autumn, the color watch is renewed, enabling you to enjoy one last period of refreshment before winter returns. But plants in winter also fascinate us, both in their stark grandeur and in the promise they hold of spring not far behind. The beauty and variety of nature inspires, refreshes and renews the human spirit.

Form

The total mass of a plant is described as form. For example, a plant's trunk, branches, and leaves together create a form. If the plant is tall and slender, it has a vertical form; if it is low and spreading, it has a horizontal form. But a group of vertical plant forms may be grouped in sufficient quantity so that the length of the group is greater than the height, the group becomes a horizontal form. A hedge of upright yews is such an example. Some shrubs with

dense foliage can be trimmed into sculptured forms called 'topiary.' This is a rather uncommon practice today because of high labor costs, but it was quite popular in seventeenth century Dutch and English gardens. Today, however, it is popular to emphasize the natural form of plants.

A good landscape design considers the form a plant takes during the full year since a plant's form can be affected by seasonal changes: in the summer a deciduous tree or shrub may have a very identifiable round or oval form, but that form will not be nearly as obvious in the winter, especially if the tree or shrub has very coarse, branching characteristics. The coarse, heavy trunk and branches may create a from of their own and dominate the winter landscape, irrespective of the summer forms originally envisioned in the composition when it was designed.

Illustrated on the next few pages are examples of plant forms. Some typical plants are named.

Fig. 6.1 *Columnar or fastigiate form: Juniper, English Oak, Lombardy Poplar, Sentry Ginkgo, Dawyck Beech.*

Fig. 6.2 *Triangular form: Juniper, Pine, Fir, Spruce, Hemlock.*

Fig. 6.3 *Round-globe (tree) form: Crabapple, Green Ash, Pistachio, Mulberry, Live Oak, Citrus, Carob, Pepper Tree.*

Fig. 6.4 *Fan-shaped form: Flowering Dogwood, Redbud, Amur Maple, Silktree, Japanese Maple.*

74

Fig. 6.5 *Broad oval form: Bradford Pear, Sugar Maple.*

Fig. 6.6 *Mounded form.*

Fig. 6.7 *Round form: Magnolia, Laurel.*

Fig. 6.8 *Oval (shrub) form.*

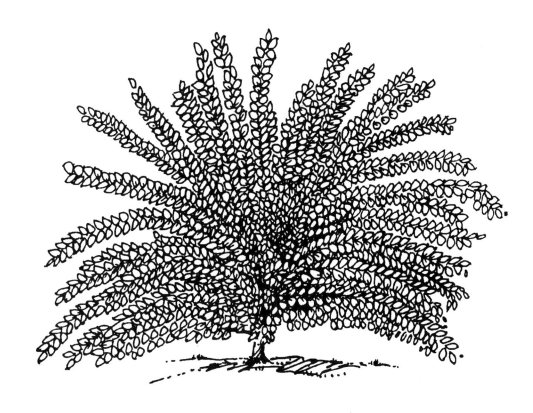

Fig. 6.9 *Mounded (shrub) form: Forsythia.*

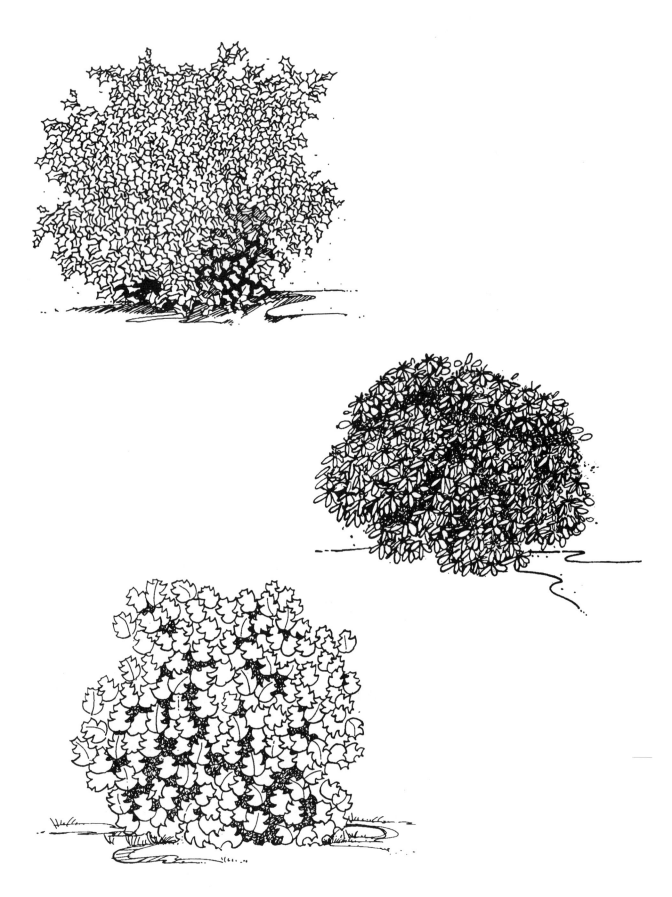

Fig. 6.10 *Round (shrub) form: Holly, Snowball, Cotoneaster, Hydrangea, Rhododendron, Azalea.*

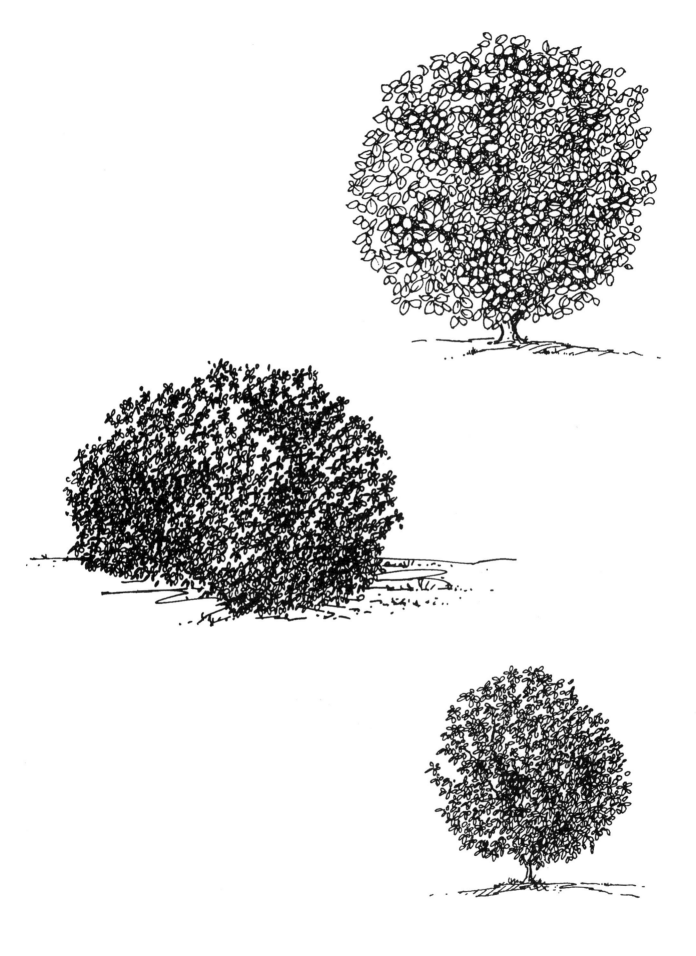

Fig. 6.11 *Horizontal form: Juniper, Cotoneaster, Bearberry, Vinca minor, Carpet Bugle, Pachysandra, Myoporum, Creeping Lantana (low shrubs and ground covers).*

Fig. 6.12 *Vines can be trained to any form.*

Fig. 6.13 *The trunks of trees are strong vertical forms in winter but almost disappear in the forest's summer foliage.*

Fig. 6.15 *Branching form of Sassafras is emphasized by a winter snow.*

Fig. 6.16 - 6.20 *Form is also expressed by the individual leaves of plants.*

Fig. 6.14 *Repetitious vertical form in a single plant.*

Fig. 6.16

Fig. 6.17

Fig. 6.18

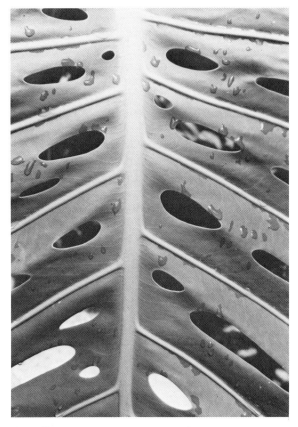

Fig. 6.19

Fig. 6.20

Textures

You should try to emphasize various textures through the use of plants and other landscape materials. The texture of plants is commonly expressed in gradations, from fine to medium to coarse. As an example, in an area to be planted with ground covers, the large leaves of Heart-leaf Bergenia (Bergenia cordifolia) are coarsely extruded in contrast to Japanese pachysandra (Pachysandra terminalis), a plant with medium texture, and Irish moss or Moss sandwort (Arenaria verna v. Caespitosa), which has a fine texture. As another contrast, pea gravel provides a fine texture against the coarse texture of a group of large (2 feet or more in diameter) boulders. Texture can also be achieved through gradations of sizes. A smaller leafed plant against any larger leafed plant provides a contrast in texture, and any three gradations of small, medium, and large leaves can be considered a change of texture in any particular composition, regardless of the particular size of the leaves involved.

Finally, texture can also be seasonal. In the winter, after the leaves have fallen, a plant covered with small leaves may look coarse, depending on the size and character of the branching, whereas a plant with somewhat larger leaves may present a rather coarse texture in the summer but a fine texture in the winter when it produces small, profuse branching.

Fig. 6.21

Fig. 6.22

Fig. 6.21 - 6.28 *Many combinations of plants provide interesting contrasts in texture. Differences are significant in some figures and subtle in others. Differences in foliage color should also be observed.*

Fig. 6.23

Fig. 6.24

Fig. 6.25

Fig. 6.26

Fig. 6.27

Fig. 6.28

85

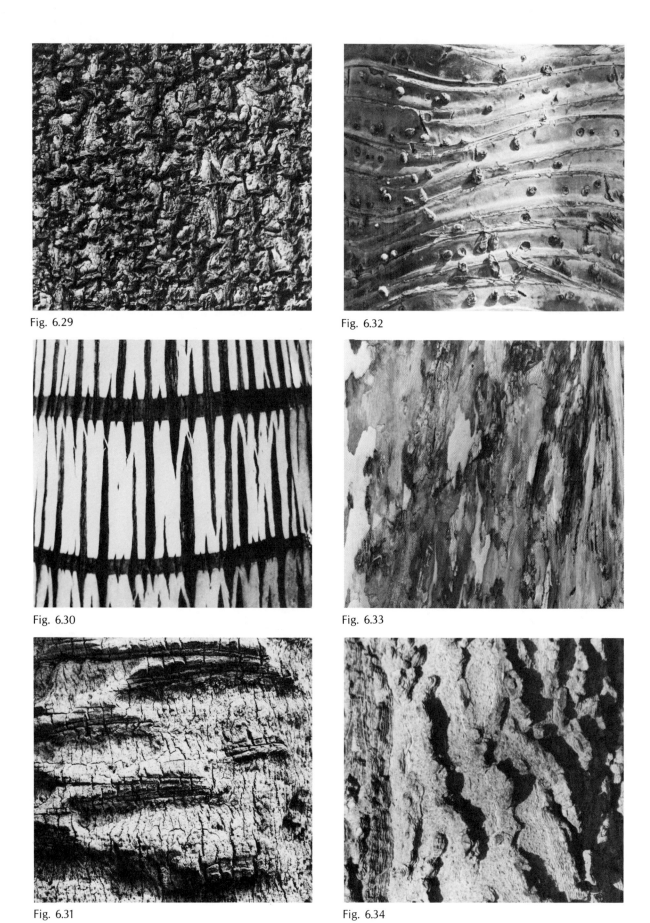

Fig. 6.29

Fig. 6.32

Fig. 6.30

Fig. 6.33

Fig. 6.31

Fig. 6.34

Fig. 6.29 - 6.34 *Texture as expressed in the bark of trees.*

Fig. 6.35

Fig. 6.36

Color

Nature's colors are nearly always superior to and more subtle than those produced by human beings. You should be sensitive to color and know how to utilize it as one of the variables in landscape design. Color has strong emotional impact on human beings. Generally, reds, oranges, and yellows are considered warm colors and seem to advance toward the viewer. Greens and blues are cooler colors and tend to recede in a composition. Dark blue, a cool color, may thus become a background color in compositions made up of several colors. Gray, being neutral, is the best background when bright colors are used in the foreground.

In the landscape, nearly everything has color, and the colors seldom seem constant. Consider the almost infinite variety of greens in leaves: even within one species the green undergoes a considerable change, from the light fresh color of an emerging leaf in spring to the darker tones of mid-summer to the complete change from green to another color when fall arrives. Flowers and fruits also provide a variety of plant color. And winter colors tend to be starker: bark's variation in color will be more noticeable and accented by the color of persistent fruit and the greens of evergreen plants.

Fig. 6.35 - 6.37 *The variety of sizes, shapes and colors of flowers add warmth and interest to the landscape.*

Fig. 6.37

87

Fig. 6.38 - 6.41 *Light foliage colors become distinctive when placed against a dark background.*

Fig. 6.40

Fig. 6.38

Fig. 6.41

Fig. 6.39

Fig. 6.42

Fig. 6.43

Fig. 6.44

Fig. 6.42 - 6.44 *Variegated plants offer contrast within their own leaf structures. They can be used in masses, or a single plant can serve as a focal point.*

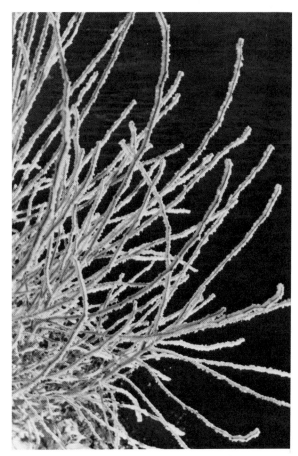

Fig. 6.45 *Frost creates strong (temporary) color contrast.*

89

Line

If you want to create or control patterns, make use of the principle of line. The lines you envision may ultimately become edges and borders. In a landscape composition a carefully planned group of lines directs the viewer's attention to a focal point or a particular area of interest. Lines are also useful in controlling visual or physical movement in straight or curved directions.

Rows of plants, such as hedges, are one example of the use of lines; a row of trees may also create a different line because of the size and character of the trees. Lines are also found in the edges of paving materials as well as in the patterns of the materials themselves. Other kinds of lines can be emphasized with fences and walls. Straight lines suggest direct movement without hesitation; interconnecting straight lines create points at their intersection for hesitation, stopping, sitting, changes of views, and reflections back to the point of beginning; and meandering lines invite slower movement and are useful in areas that should seem as natural as possible, such as paths through woods.

Fig. 6.47 *Flower beds and shrub masses have been used to create curvilinear line.*

Fig. 6.48 *Plants which may be vertical as individuals create a horizontal form or line when used as a hedge.*

Fig. 6.46 *When trees are planted in rows such as for windbreaks, lines are created. Lombardy Poplar, shown here, makes an especially strong line.*

Fig. 6.49 *This planting lacks repetition, harmony and unity.*

Fig. 6.50 *Without any change in texture or foliage color, a planting can be monotonous.*

Fig. 6.51 *Repetition of plants with the same form, color and texture create unified masses.*

Variety

A critical element in design is variety: too little is monotonous, and too much is confusing. A very fine balance between these extremes produces a pleasant sense of unity in a landscape composition. For example, planting design containing only junipers — even though junipers have a variety of forms and sizes — can be monotonous because the texture of junipers is so uniform. A variety of plant forms, textures, and colors is needed to create an orderly, interesting landscape composition. This does not mean, however, that every shrub and every tree must be different within a design.

Repetition

Repetition provides variety, meaning, and expression. It reduces the confusion that may result from excessive variety, introducing a sense of order to viewers of the landscape. Designers frequently use the word 'order' to describe a pleasing design. Repetition is usually achieved by placing individual plants of a single species in groups or masses. This results in a repetition of the individual plant's form, texture, and color. In a large-scale landscape, these masses of varying sizes may be repeated as you find necessary. In a small, landscape area you should have less repetition and greater variety; in larger areas you will need considerably more repetition and less variety to prevent confusion.

Fig. 6.52 *Repetition of rounded forms creates harmony even though there is contrasting texture and foliage color.*

Balance

Visualize a central axis in your landscape composition. If weight, numbers, masses, and so on are distributed equally on both sides of the central axis, the composition is in balance. It is on the basis of balance that landscapes are considered formal (symmetrical) or informal (asymmetrical). In a formal landscape the distribution on either side of the axis is likely to be the same, plant by plant. Except for a few public gardens, there are now few formal landscape designs because since World War II informality has been more popular. In informal landscapes the balance is equivalent rather than exact; a large plant on one side of the axis may balance with a number of smaller plants on the other side. It is not nearly as difficult for painters to achieve balance on their canvasses as it will be for you, the designer of the landscape, because the landscape can be walked through and viewed from several different positions, while the painter only contends with a two-dimensional surface. The problem of balance thus is quite complex, and you should keep this in mind when you are arranging the plants and other materials as various elements in the composition. If you are not careful, the composition may be in balance from one or two views but out of balance from a third position.

Emphasis

Through the use of emphasis the eye is directed to one portion or object, the focal point. The focal point can be a single tree, a group of shrubs with unique character, or a structural feature like a fountain. Secondary points of interest may be used also to direct the eye toward plants or other landscape features that have less contrast with the overall composition than does a primary focal point. Other examples of focal points or areas or emphasis in the planting includes a single plant of white or of vivid colors in an otherwise green composition, a red-leaved tree or shrub among a group of green plantings, or a very coarse, large plant among a mass planting of fine-textured ground covers.

PLANT MASSES

Transition

You should try to achieve a transition from plant mass to plant mass in your design. For example relate large vertical plant masses to horizontal plants. Or create pyramidal effect by using smaller plants in front of larger ones so that the total plant mass will descend in size from the largest plant to the smallest. This technique also covers unsightly bare spots that sometimes occur at the base of large

Fig. 6.53 *This planting composition is an example of asymmetrical balance. Horizontal masses are formed by using multiple quantities of each plant (repetition) which progresses from lowest in front to tallest in rear (pyramidal effect).*

92

Fig. 6.54 *Center plant is a strong focal point.*

Fig. 6.55

Fig. 6.56

Fig. 6.55- 6.56 *Unusual branching patterns can serve as focal points.*

shrubs, especially as the shrubs mature. You can also use the descending pyramidal effect in isolated, large masses to make a gradual transition from a high point in the center of the mass to a low level at the edges of the mass. Large plant masses usually have a most pleasant effect if they are viewed from a distance, but large plant masses, especially if they are not pyramidal, on both sides of a pedestrian corridor produce an uncomfortably crowded feeling among people.

Change in topography, in conjunction with the changes in the height of plant masses, creates pleasing dimensional variations in the landscape. Consider using earth mounds or land sculpture to heighten the awareness of dimension in the planting design.

You should also try to provide transition in texture. Abrupt changes from fine to coarse textures within a single plant mass is not as aesthetically pleasing as a gradual transition because the difference in texture emphasize the individuality of the plants rather than the unity of the entire plant mass. How often such transitions should occur depends on the size of the project and the effect you want. For example, in a small garden you can use very coarsely textured plants as the focal point, with gradual texture transitions between other plant masses so as to not attract the eye away from the point of emphasis. In a very large garden, the point of emphasis can be a very large mass of plants or a grouping of objects. The gradual textural transition throughout all subordinate plant masses may then be more important than a transition within each individual mass of plants. If you love plants, you may want more different individual plants than you can effectively group together in a harmonious design. One way to visually unify or tie together this assortment is to use a facing plant of lower mass in front of the other various plants. For example, say you have a group of six medium- and large-sized shrubs, all of a different genus and species. A species of a small-sized plant in front of the six plants unifies the entire group.

You can achieve seasonal stability yet still have variety by planting a mix of deciduous plants or conifers or broad-leaved evergreens. Deciduous plants lose their leaves each fall and regrow them when spring arrives. Conifer plants typically have needles, such as pine, spruce, hemlock and fir. Most conifers are evergreen, except the Larch, which is a deciduous conifer that loses its needles each fall and regrows them in the spring. Climate and the hardiness of individual plants, as well as plant availability, will dictate the possibility of mixing plants within a particular composition. For instance, there is a greater choice of broad-leaved evergreens

93

in warm climates, but in cold climates the deciduous materials will probably dominate, with the evergreens being principally coniferous. Rarely should any design composition consist totally of either evergreen or deciduous plants; you should have a mix of both. If you must keep costs to a minimum, remember that deciduous plants are less expensive and grow faster than evergreens.

Leaf color can also add interest to plant masses. The gradation can be very subtle when based on plants' textures; or the color of an individual plant such as the Japanese Red Maple (Acer palmatum v. artropurpurea), can be the focal point because it has a dramatic enough leaf color. In recent years many varieties of plants with variegated leaves have been developed; these varieties have a transition of color within each individual leaf in a plant. Such plants are quite attractive and can be used rather effectively in a composition, especially as a focal point. By the careful selection of plants you can plant for flower color that changes in sequence amount the individual plants of the large mass. Flowering may begin in early spring, continue through most of the season, and then terminate in the fall, with leaves turning color in those portions of the country where plants acquire a fall color. One such plant is the Winged Euonymous (Euonymous alatus), whose leaves turn a bright crimson.

Scale

You must always consider design effects in relation to the scale (size) of the landscape area. For example, you can get more variety and less repetition in a small garden by using smaller masses of plants. In small-scale areas the viewing distance is short, so greater detail in individual plants and the subtleness in the flowers' color can be observed at close range. Plant fragrances are more important in small areas than in large areas because people can detect and enjoy the fragrances that are close at hand. But individual plants form masses in and of themselves in small areas, and repetition, if overdone, can easily lead to monotony. Also, a plant such as the Colorado Blue Spruce is too large in a small-scale area, and overwhelms other plants as well as viewers. Other, less massive trees are available that rise above a person and provide welcome shade and shelter.

Specific Design Problems

Many problems can be solved by using a wide selection of plants. By anticipating all possible problems ahead of time, you can devise a landscape design that will eliminate these problems before they occur.

The location of plants can be quite a dilemma. Nurseries sell small plants that grow and grow and

Fig. 6.57 *Leaves of Japanese Red Maple*

Fig. 6.58 *Maidenhair fern, focal point for small scale design.*

Fig. 6.59 *A large flower can be a temporary focal point.*

Fig. 6.60

Fig. 6.61

Fig. 6.60 - 6.61 *Plants which grow too large are soon out of scale for their surroundings. The composition is out of balance and lacks interest.*

grow. You must plan on spacing plants apart and away from structures according to their ultimate growth; otherwise, many years from now plants may be too close together. Homeowners often fail to consider ultimate growth, opting instead for the immediate effect of plants nicely clumped together, and selecting plants that are potentially much too large for the spaces they must occupy. Pruning will become more necessary and frequent, and in some cases the plantings will crowd the sidewalk or patio, making it difficult and uncomfortable to use these facilities. Crowding also decreases the longevity of plants, which means that you will have to replace plants sooner than you expected.

Other concerns you must keep in mind are the shade and growth requirements plants need at both the time of their installation and 10 to 15 years later. For example, a shade-requiring ground cover, such as pachysandra, may not survive under what may become a large shade tree because initially the tree is not large enough to provide the sun protection the pachysandra needs. You may have to consider a plant's transition from being sun tolerant to shade tolerant. Conversely, many sun-loving shrubs may grow well and look good during their early years, but as trees grow and provide more and more shade, the shrubs will come spindly, thin, unsightly, and fail to flower and fruit.

Maintenance can also be a problem when ground cover is planted among roses or other thorny shrubs because pulling weeds around them is painful and frustrating. A fourth problem is narrow or crowded spaces and unsightly surfaces. Use vines in these situations, especially where you want a plant that will be leafy yet grow to a great height. Vines are good on tall walls or on a structure where there is a narrow planting space between the structure and sidewalk. Vines also climb unsightly power poles and television towers. Fences too can be covered by vines; you can make good use of changes in color and texture by using Boston Ivy on a light brick or stone wall. When space allows, a facing of junipers will provide additional texture and color contrast. Finally, you can create shade in limited space by directing vines on garden structures, porches, and so on.

Remember to plan carefully for grassy areas. When beech or other trees with low-spreading branches are planted in open lawns, the grass will not survive. Sparsely leafed and high-branching trees, like thornless. Honey Locust, are more desirable when you want a luxuriant lawn because they let more light filter through to the grass below. In Southern California, Hawaii, and Florida, palm trees provide light shade.

Also consider the color contrasts that are necessary when you design for planting against walls and fences. Yews will not show up nearly as well against a red brick wall as they will against a buff brick or white cast stone wall. A Silver or Blue Juniper provides better contrast against red brick. Some trees are notorious for their surface roots. This can be an especially troublesome problem in heavy clay soils. If you plant such trees too close to paving, the roots will eventually heave the paving upward, creating safety and aesthetic problems.

FUNCTIONAL QUALITIES OF PLANTS

Often plants are referred to as ornamentals, but as you will discover from the following discussion, plants are also functional. It may be hard for you to separate the functional and aesthetic qualities of plants, but remember that these qualities work together in the landscape design.

Visual Control

Plants can be very effective barriers or screens, providing privacy and eliminating such objectionable scenes or views as junk yards or trash areas. They can direct the view of an observer or frame the most desirable view in a particular direction. Plants can also help define a particular space, such as a vegetable garden, separating it from the home, deck, patio, or other area.

It is also possible to create outdoor 'rooms,' with turf or lawn as the floor, screen planting forming walls, and a canopy of trees overhead as the roof. To provide privacy, plantings should be at least 6 feet high. Remember that you cannot create such rooms immediately: it takes several years for trees to grow high enough to provide a roof or canopy. Plantings for privacy or rooms need not be monotonous. A hedge of one particular plant is effective but can be boring; less-formal screen plantings may include a sufficient variety of materials, artistically arranged to create a very pleasant appearance.

Fig. 6.62 *Vines can be used to soften the stark appearance of, as well as to add shading to, large expanses of walls.*

Fig. 6.63 *Palms provide light shade and interesting shadow patterns.*

96

Fig. 6.64 *Outdoor rooms compare to indoor rooms.*

SCREENING PLANT MATERIALS

Fig. 6.65 *Various heights of screen planting. For visual screen use materials above eye level.*

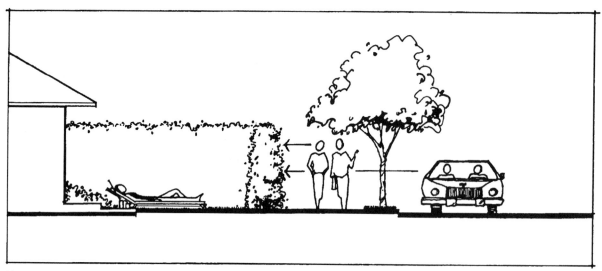

Fig. 6.66 *Hedges can be used to screen small spaces.*

PRIVACY CREATED BETWEEN
BUILDING AND PLANTING

Fig. 6.67 *Visual screening.*

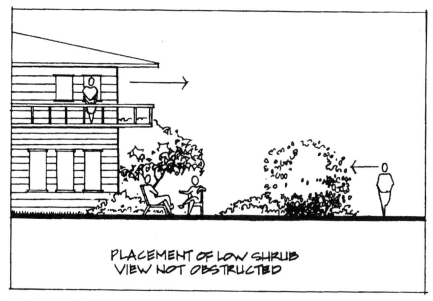

PLACEMENT OF LOW SHRUB
VIEW NOT OBSTRUCTED

Fig. 6.68 *Visual screening with a view over.*

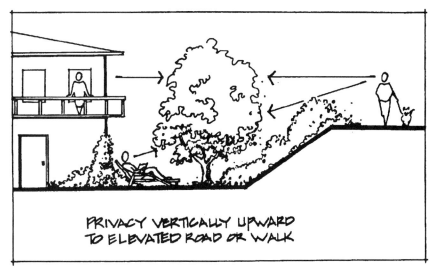

Fig. 6.69 *Visual screening.*

Fig. 6.70 *Visual screening with a view over.*

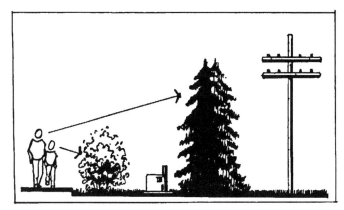

Fig. 6.71 *Screen garbage and utility areas.*

Plants can reduce or control the visual discomfort caused by glare or reflection. Glare can come from such sources as the sun, street lights, automobile headlights, and signs. Reflected light is indirect light or light that has bounced off of some surface, such as a body of water, like a lake or reflecting pool, or adjacent paving surface. Light is also commonly reflected from large glass surfaces on a structure or from snow.

You should identify any sources of glare and reflected light and then use planting to minimize these two problems. The most effective control of stationary glare is to locate plantings, as close as possible to the area from which the light shines. However, plants too close to light posts or utility wires may be butchered by unskilled pruning crews from the power company. The natural shapes of the plants will be destroyed, and some species may die from unattended wounds.

To control reflected light, intercept the light before it reaches its destination. Plantings adjacent to the edge of water bodies will prevent the reflected light from reaching any areas behind the screen planting. Large canopies of trees over paved surfaces prevent the sun from reaching the paving and causing light reflection back into adjacent windows or sitting areas. You must carefully place trees over paved areas to keep light reflection to its absolute minimum. A tree like the Honey Locust provides a filtered kind of light that is sufficient to reduce reflection but not so heavy as to heavily shade the entire paved area.

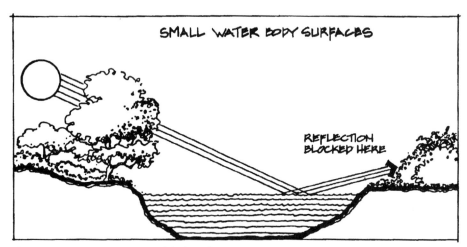

Fig. 6.72a *Screening to control light reflection.*

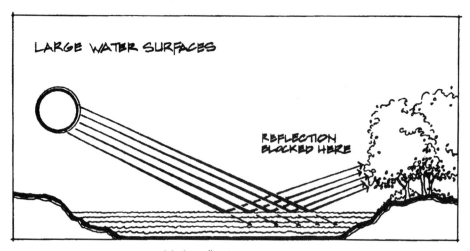

Fig. 6.72b *Screening to control light reflection.*

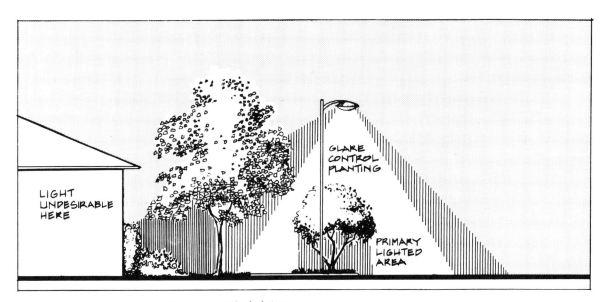

Fig. 6.73 *Planting to control glare from night lighting.*

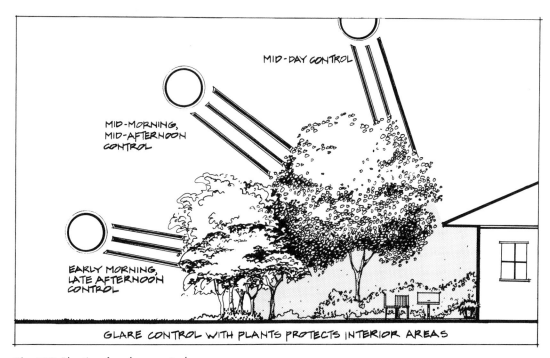

Fig. 6.74 *Planting for glare control.*

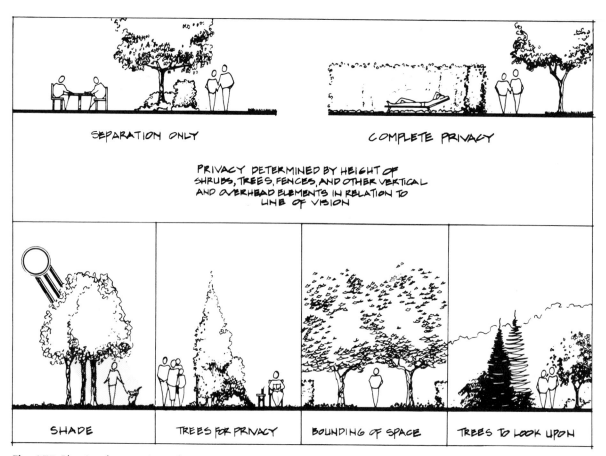

SEPARATION ONLY

COMPLETE PRIVACY

PRIVACY DETERMINED BY HEIGHT OF
SHRUBS, TREES, FENCES, AND OTHER VERTICAL
AND OVERHEAD ELEMENTS IN RELATION TO
LINE OF VISION

SHADE

TREES FOR PRIVACY

BOUNDING OF SPACE

TREES TO LOOK UPON

Fig. 6.75 *Planting for a variety of situations.*

SMALL TREE WILL NOT
INTERFERE WITH UTILITY
POLE WIRES

PYRAMIDAL TREE

COLUMNAR TREE

Fig. 6.76 *Planting near utilities.*

You can achieve immediate privacy by installing fences or other structural features, but these are usually the most expensive solutions. Plants provide a less expensive, more pleasant, less rigid kind of screen planting if the space is available. Be patient: it will take longer to achieve privacy with plants than with fences.

Physical Barriers

The movement of people and animals can be effectively controlled by plants. Low plantings, 3 feet or less in height, provide only a certain amount of control, more psychological than physical, especially for adults. Young adults and children, as well as animals, fine low plantings inviting to jump over and run through. Plantings between 3 to 6 feet high offer a bit more control; those that are thick or contain thorns and briars are the most effective in this height range, although teenagers will try almost anything on a dare.

Thick and solid planting 6 feet or taller are adequate for both physical and visual control. You can use plants in place of fences as a physical barrier, or use them in masses along sidewalks to direct people toward some desired location and to help prevent the unnecessary destruction of turf areas resulting from people walking across them as shortcuts. (See Fig. 6.79)

Climate Control

The various climatic factors that effect human comfort are solar radiation, air temperature, air movement (wind), precipitation, and humidity. Human comfort is a result of the favorable interrelationships of these factors. There are, of course, some rather narrow limits in which people can be considered comfortable, although this varies somewhat from people to people and from geographical area to geographical area. Plants may modify some of these conditions in certain situations and help provide the desired comfort level. For example, plants can be effective wind barriers and can reduce solar radiation and temperature by shading, thus assisting in energy conservation.

If your home is one of several placed together on a site such as in a subdivision, the wind intensity between buildings and coming around certain corners can become very intense, depending on the wind's direction. Carefully placed plantings can reduce the effects of this wind. In the Midwest, a windbreak of Scotch pine can be effective. Evergreen plants provide year-round wind protection. For small properties, closely placed plants can provide a very tight mass, like a hedge.

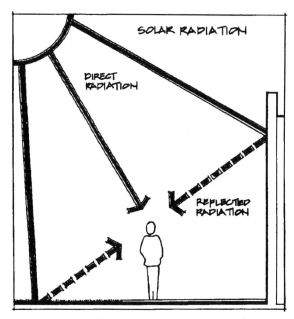
Fig. 6.77 *Solar radiation arrives from several directions.*

Fig. 6.78 *Planting to reduce solar radiation.*

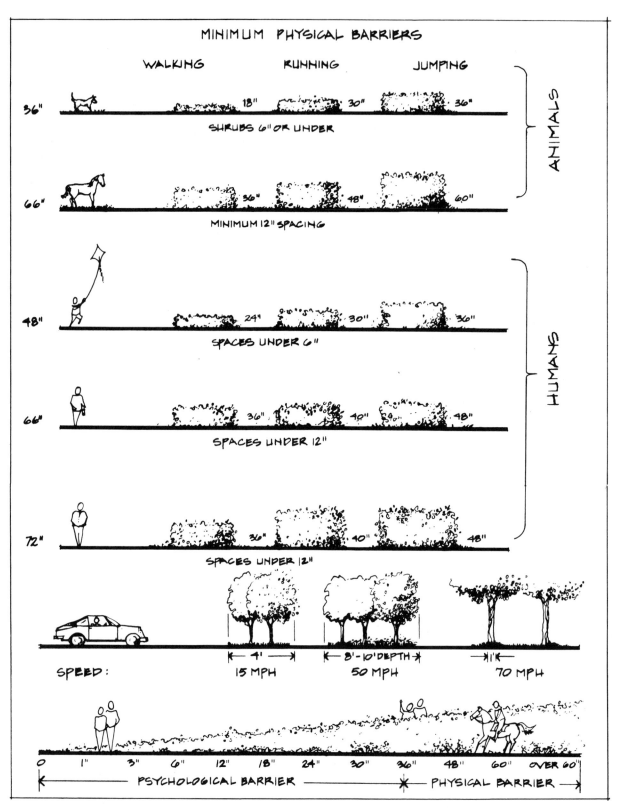

Fig. 6.79 *Sizes of minimum physical barriers.*

104

Wind creates a chill factor that reduces human comfort during cool months. You have to consider the height of the windbreak in the area that has to be protected. Use the densest plantings adjacent to the area to be protected for the greatest wind reduction. Less dense plantings provide less immediate wind control but can sometimes reduce its overall effect over a longer distance. In climates where winter, spring, and fall chilling is not a factor but wind is desired for cooling, use plants to help funnel wind into the desired areas. For year-round wind protection, include evergreen plantings in the wind screen.

Fig. 6.80 *A planting mass forces air up and over.*

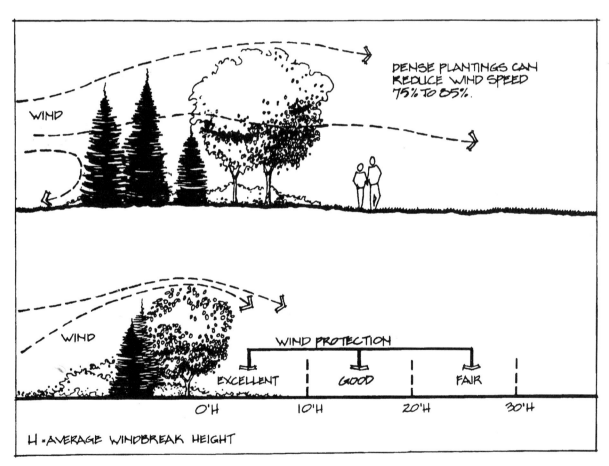

DENSE PLANTINGS CAN REDUCE WIND SPEED 75% TO 85%.

WIND

WIND

WIND PROTECTION

EXCELLENT   GOOD   FAIR

0'H   10'H   20'H   30'H

H = AVERAGE WINDBREAK HEIGHT

Fig. 6.81 *Windbreaks provide protection. If a windbreak is 20 feet high, it will provide excellent protection as far as 200 feet, or 10 x H when H=20.*

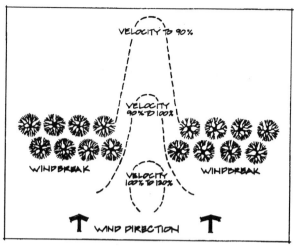

Fig. 6.82 *Wind velocity increases in a windbreak gap much as it does between large buildings in a city.*

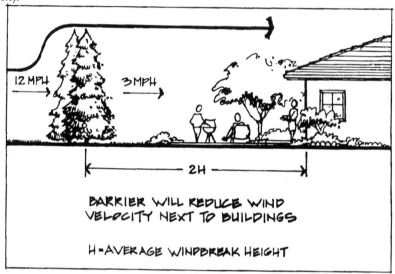

Fig. 6.83 *Planting for wind reduction around the home.*

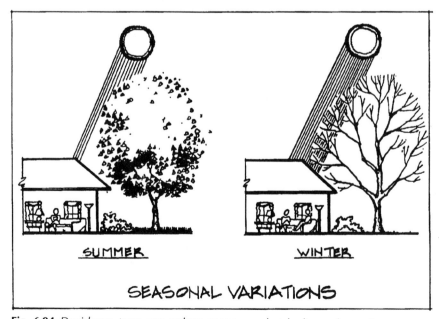

Fig. 6.84 *Deciduous trees can reduce energy use by shading a home in summer and allowing solar radiation to penetrate in winter.*

Shade

The nature of the soil and paving surfaces greatly determines just how much solar radiation is absorbed and how much is reflected into the surrounding air affecting the temperature. Asphalt, which is dark, greatly absorbs solar radiation and increases the air temperature around it. Concrete reflects more of the light rather than absorbing it. In terms of plants, a canopy of trees reflects back into the sky more of the incoming solar radiation and thus reduces the temperature level underneath the trees. This is why trees are so useful in providing shade and increasing human comfort.

Plants also re-radiate at night, very quickly releasing the heat energy stored during the day. Asphalt and concrete release very slowly. Thus wooded areas or forests are much cooler at night than paved urban areas. If your home is underneath a canopy of trees, it will be cooler in both the daytime and the nighttime, reducing the need for air conditioning and subsequently saving you energy costs. If the canopy of trees is deciduous, your home can absorb some of the solar radiation during the cooler time of the year.

Precipitation and Humidity Control

Although plants are not waterproof shelters, they do provide some immediate and temporary shelter from rain. A considerable amount of precipitation has to collect on trees' foliage before the moisture begins to pass through the foliage to the ground below. Properly located semi-penetrable planting barriers can also prevent snow drifts on driveways and sidewalks. The placement of the barrier is determined by the direction of the prevailing winter wind (determined in your site analysis). In the Midwest the prevailing winter wind is from the northwest, so generally the snow barriers are placed along the western edge of properties. This lumps most of the snow along the back side of the property. A solid barrier dumps the snow farther in, away from the barrier, than a semi-penetrable one that allows some movement through it. Thus a solid wall along the property will move the snow farther into the yard. A solid evergreen windbreak therefore is not necessarily the best snow drift barrier if you want to keep the snow close to the barrier. A combination of evergreens for wind control and deciduous trees and shrubs for snow control is the best solution.

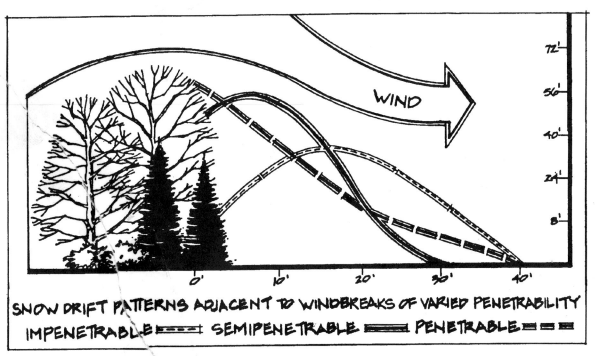

Fig. 6.85 Snow drift patterns adjacent to windbreaks of varied penetrability.

Plants contain large quantities of water that they release into the air through the process of transpiration. The greater the amount of foliage (as in oaks, maples, beech, and ash), the greater the amount of water added to the air. This natural form of air conditioning is especially effective in climates where the summer air humidity is low; it is less effective in areas of higher humidity.

Noise Control

Noise and sound can be somewhat controlled by plants, depending upon the thickness of the foliage, the size of the branches, and the loudness of the sound, its position, and its frequency in relation to the listener. Mounds of plants attenuate sound much better than rows of plants, so when the intensity of the sound or noise is such that considerable attenuation is needed, then mounding with plants on top is a good design solution. If your property is located where noise is a particular problem for you, you may want to consult with an acoustical engineer who has had experience in outdoor sound attenuation. Or, because vertical walls are better sound attenuators than plants, where space is limited, consider the use of a solid brick or stone wall to partially shut out noise that may be adjacent to you.

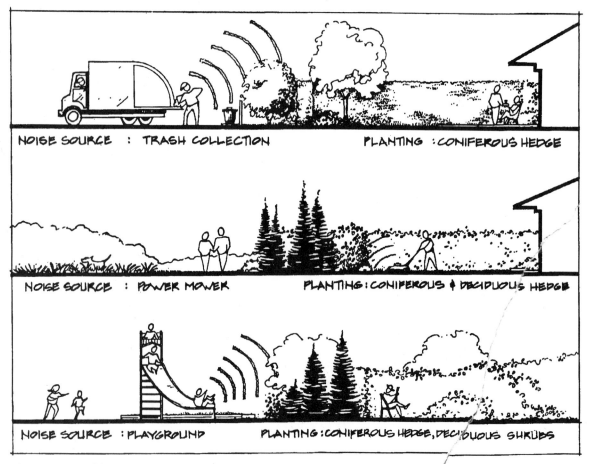

NOISE SOURCE : TRASH COLLECTION   PLANTING : CONIFEROUS HEDGE

NOISE SOURCE : POWER MOWER   PLANTING : CONIFEROUS & DECIDUOUS HEDGE

NOISE SOURCE : PLAYGROUND   PLANTING : CONIFEROUS HEDGE, DECIDUOUS SHRUBS

Fig. 6.86a *Visual barriers to noise sources.*

Fig. 6.86b *A planting of conifers on a mound can significantly reduce the noise of vehicular traffic.*

PLANTING : DECIDUOUS
NOISE REDUCTION : AUTO 50%, TRUCK 75%

PLANTING : CONIFEROUS
NOISE REDUCTION : AUTO 75%, TRUCK 80%

Fig. 6.86c *Effects of deciduous and coniferous plantings on noise reduction.*

Erosion Control

Nearly every time a new home is built and the surrounding ground is disturbed, erosion becomes a serious problem. Often, during construction (and immediately thereafter) valuable topsoil and some subsoil are lost, especially where rainfall is heavy. The use of plants is one of the most effective ways to control erosion; establishing them early in your landscape will prevent further topsoil loss. Plants help reduce the impact of rain upon the soil, and the roots hold the soil particles together, preventing them from washing away. And because plants tend to hold water in place, they also help reduce runoff and increase water penetration into the subsoil where it can be utilized. Generally, grass is the quickest and easiest vegetation that can be planted for erosion control. On slopes where permanent plantings are to be established place heavy mulches (rather than grass) around the base of the plants to help control erosion until the plantings have become firmly established. Such plantings can include low-growing ground covers.

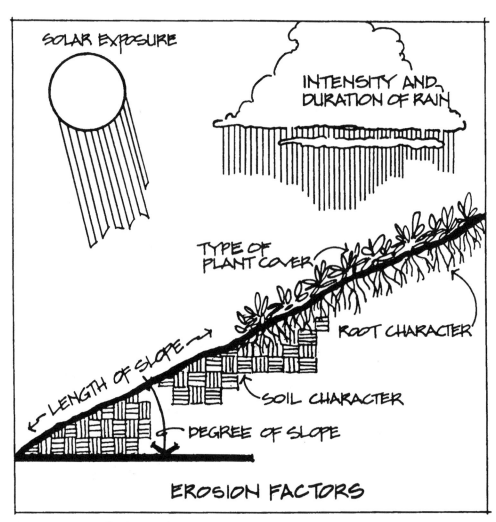

Fig. 6.87 *Factors affecting erosion.*

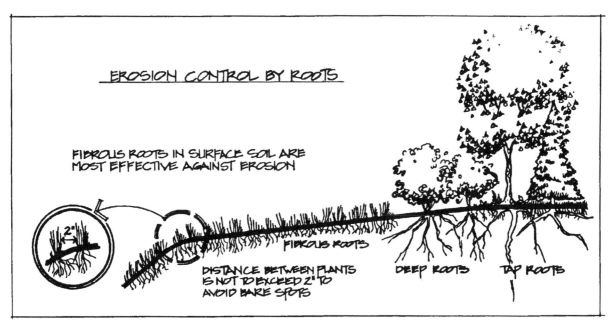

Fig. 6.88 *Plants can help control erosion.*

Fig. 6.89 *Planting combined with pre-cast concrete and stone riprap can be used for erosion control on steep slopes.*

Wildlife Habitats

In recent years home dwellers have become much more conscious of the total quality of the environment. This includes the survival habitats wild life needs, especially in urban areas. A number of plants are useful for providing food and shelter for birds and other wildlife, such as chipmunks, squirrels, rabbits, and deer. Such plants must yield fruits and nuts, which are food for birds and animals.

Table 6-1 A selection of plants that attract birds.

Botanical	Common name
EASTERN	
Celastrus scandens	Bittersweet
Cornus spp.	Dogwood
Crataegus spp.	Hawthorn
Elaeagnus umellata	Autumn-olive
Ilex spp.	Holly
Juniperus virginiana	Eastern red-cedar
Lonicera maackii	Amur honeysuckle
Lonicera tatarica	Tatarian honeysuckle
Malus spp.	Crabapple
Parthenocissus quinquefolia	Virginia creeper
Prunus spp.	Cherry
Pyracantha spp.	Firethorn
Rhus spp.	Sumac
Sorbus spp.	Mountain-ash
Vaccinium corymbosum	Highbush blueberry
Viburnum trilobum	American cranberrybush
WESTERN	
Amelanchier spp.	Shadbush
Arbutus menziesii	Madrone
Berberis spp.	Barberry
Fremontodendron californica	Fremontia or flannelbush
Garrya elliptica	Coast silk-tassel
Heteromeles arbutifolia	Toyon
Mahonia spp.	Mahonia
Myrica californica	Wax-myrtle
Prunus spp.	Cherry
Rhus spp.	Sumac
Ribes spp.	Currant, gooseberry Sambucus
spp.	Elderberry
Symphoricarpos spp.	Snowberry, coralberry

PLANT LIST

Plants are living materials. They need food, water, soil, air and light to grow and develop. When you understand their needs they will grow better with fewer problems and you will be more satisfied with the results.

Some plants are utilized as food by certain insects and animals, and you will need to know how to protect your plants against them. There are also disease to guard against.

Plants which grow well in one geographic area will be frequently not thrive in another because of differences in soils and climate. Acid loving plants cannot tolerate the alkaline soils of the Western United States. Broad leafed evergreens which enjoy living in Tennessee cannot tolerate the cold winters of Minnesota.

In order to effectively design with plants and prepare a planting plan, you need to create a plant list. The plants you use should be hardy for your area. Many catalogs and books refer to hardiness zone and a United States map of these hardiness zones is included here for your information. Locate your zone from the map. If you are on the border between zones, it is safest to select the lower number, or colder zone.

How can you find out which plants are hardy for your area and will tolerate your particular soils and climate? There are several possibilities. Inquire at local nurseries for lists they may be using themselves. Look up any arboretums or botanical gardens nearby. Colleges with horticulture or botany departments may use part of the campus as a mini-arboretum. Check with local libraries for any books produced locally and contact your state extension horticulturist at your state land-grant university. In Appendix C you will find a listing of state nursery associations and some books about plants.

With the suggestions you get, build a list by taking a snapshot of each plant seen (or clipping from a catalog), and paste it on a sheet with the following information alongside:

1. Botanical or Scientific name
2. Common name (may have more than one)
3. Height and Spread (average mature size)
4. Evergreen or deciduous
5. Foliage color by season
6. Flowers (size and color)
7. Fruit (size and color)
8. Form (rounded, columnar, oval, etc.)
9. Texture (coarse, medium, fine)
10. Exposure needed (sun, shade, partial shade)
11. Disease, insect susceptibility
12. Miscellaneous (thorns, strong flower odors, nuts attract wildlife, etc.).

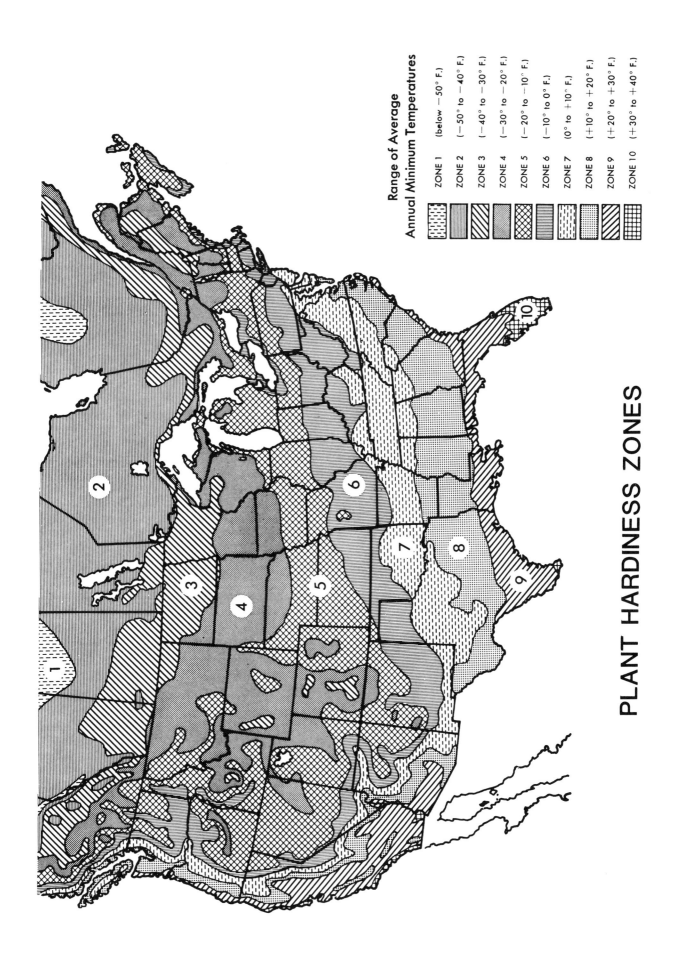

Range of Average
Annual Minimum Temperatures

ZONE 1 (below −50° F.)
ZONE 2 (−50° to −40° F.)
ZONE 3 (−40° to −30° F.)
ZONE 4 (−30° to −20° F.)
ZONE 5 (−20° to −10° F.)
ZONE 6 (−10° to 0° F.)
ZONE 7 (0° to +10° F.)
ZONE 8 (+10° to +20° F.)
ZONE 9 (+20° to +30° F.)
ZONE 10 (+30° to +40° F.)

PLANT HARDINESS ZONES

113

Construction Techniques

7

With a basic understanding of materials and how they work together, the homeowner can create many interesting landscape features. Any limitation besides the material itself will include factors like installation techniques, cost, maintenance problems, and temperature fluctuations, including frost action.

You will need to be aware of any local zoning regulations or building codes which will restrict your activity. You may be required to obtain a building permit for fences, decks, shelters and so on. The placement of these items in relation to your property line may be restricted both as to height and distance from the line. These codes may be administered slightly differently in each state, county or city, and administrative offices can vary in location from the planning department to the city/county engineer's office. In addition to building codes, even further restrictions may have been recorded in your property deed by the developer of your property. Some developments require that homeowners submit plans for any improvements to their property for review and approval by a committee before construction begins. On your own property be aware of the location of any underground or overhead utilities before you begin digging or erecting poles that may interrupt service or worse, cause you injury or electrocution. Utility companies will gladly let you know if potential problems exist, free of charge.

PAVING

Paving provides a solid surface underfoot and covers up the soil or gravel underneath it. It can be considered one of the nicer amenities of civilization. Too much paving is drab looking, but with a little thought and a little planning the aesthetic appearance of new paving can be greatly improved. Many of the illustrations in this chapter and Chapter 5 can provide ideas for the different ways paving can be used in landscaping.

The aggregates used in concrete and asphalt paving are generally readily available from local gravel pits; only the portland and asphalt cements have to be sent from other locations. These paving materials are generally the least expensive depending how much work you do yourself. Asphalt placing will need to be contracted out as it is not a project for the homeowner. It will be more expensive than concrete paving you lay yourself and, depending on the current price of brick or pre-cast pavers, may be more expensive than these if you install them yourself. Most flat surface concrete can be installed easily, requiring only a minimum of hand labor. However, it is heavy work and you need to be in good physical condition to handle it. It is much easier if you have some help as it is very difficult to handle yourself, especially for large areas like a driveway. You will want to enlist the help of some friends or neighbors with whom you can trade labor.

Much hand labor is involved in installing brick, stone, and pre-cast pavers, this greatly increasing the cost of these pavements in contrast to concrete. But if you are willing to develop your skills and use your own time, you can install rather expensive looking pavements at a minimum cost since you do not have to pay for professional labor. And you can save more of your time by laying brick or stone on sand, which is the easiest paving method and enables you to work at your own pace, whereas once concrete is poured it must be worked until completion.

Asphalt and Concrete

As mentioned in Chapter 4 and earlier in this chapter, asphalt paving involves specialized equipment — it is better to hire a contractor to lay the asphalt.

Working with Concrete. The forms for concrete can be 2 x 4s for most projects, but if you are going to use a 5-inch depth for a concrete driveway then a 2 x 6 will be better. Gentle curves can be formed with 1/4 inch plywood while sheet steel can be used for sharper curves. Forms should be staked with 1 x 2s or 2 x 2s no further than 4 feet apart, but stakes as close as 12 inches may be needed on curves to provide sufficient support to keep the shape of the curve. Use a minimum of 4 feet in width for walks so two people can walk side by side. For drives a 10-foot width is necessary for one car and 16 feet for two cars. These widths provide for the opening and closing of doors and allow passengers to leave the car and step directly onto the pavement.

To estimate the amount of concrete you will need, figure one cubic yard of concrete to cover 81 square feet to a depth of 4 inches and 65 square feet at a depth of 5 inches. One cubic yard equals 27 cubic feet. As concrete hardens, you must make sure you keep it moist for 7 days. Cover the concrete with plastic sheeting. In those sections of the country subject to freezing temperatures it is best to use air-entrained concrete purchased from your local ready-mix plant for all paving areas. This will provide you with a paving surface less subject to frost and ice damage and deterioration. If you live in a warmer climate or decide to mix your own concrete for footings and so forth, you may want to rent a mixer from the local tool rental store. You will probably need access to a small truck to haul or pull the mixer and secure your gravel, sand, cement, forming supplies, reinforcing steel and so forth from various suppliers. The advantage of mixing your own gives you the option of mixing small quantities at a time and spreading the work over several days or weeks.

Thus, the work can be done on weekends and holidays. Most ready-mix plants have minimum orders and you will need to plan your work to use this minimum. If you order ready-mix, specify that the quality be at least a mix of six sacks of cement per cubic yard and have a 4-inch slump. The physical demands may be heavy and extra help needed to meet the challenge. Concrete should not be poured in freezing weather. To be safe, avoid doing any work when the temperature falls below 40 degrees. Also avoid pouring concrete when the temperature rises above 90 degrees as it will be difficult to finish before it sets up.

It is important that you have a good base under your paving to prevent it from heaving during freeze-thaw cycles. For concrete paving you should have from 5 to 10 inches of compacted pit run gravel. This type of gravel is a mix of gravel and sand which when slightly moist can be compacted very tightly to prevent water from accumulating under the pavement. The best compaction is done with a small power compactor which you can rent from your local tool rental dealer. It is run by a small gasoline engine and pushed around by one person while it vibrates a flat plate over the surface of the gravel. The individual gravel and sand particles are pounded together and air spaces eliminated. The soil underneath your gravel base should be the original undisturbed soil. If during the past five years it has been filled through other construction activity around your home and is any way unstable, it must be compacted before you place your gravel base. If the unstable area is more than 6 inches deep, then you will need to excavate to the original undisturbed level and compact the soil in 6-inch layers up to the level where you add your base. Only in this manner can you be assured of having a stable paving surface that will not settle. Such soil should be free from organic debris such as leaves, grass, twigs and so forth. Clay soils which are too wet or too dry will not compact well.

Drainage is crucial for all paving surfaces to prevent moisture accumulation, facilitate early drying (and use of the surface), and reduce frost damage. This drainage slope should not be less than 1/8 inch drop in every foot horizontally. If you have a 24-inch spirit level, this would mean that with one end of the level resting on the pavement, the other end should be at least 1/4 inch above the pavement surface when the bubble reads in the middle position of the level.

Most concrete should be reinforced with steel to help prevent cracking. This is especially true for driveways and any other areas where vehicular traffic will go. Large patios poured with few joints will also hold up better with reinforcing. Patios with wood

Fig. 7.1 *An example of exposed aggregate and broom finish concrete paving used together. Direction of brooming is alternated with each panel.*

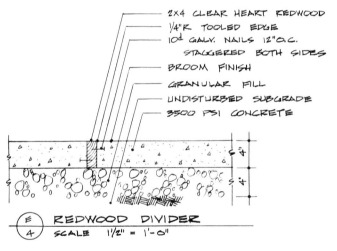

2X4 CLEAR HEART REDWOOD
1/4"R TOOLED EDGE
10d GALV. NAILS 12"O.C.
STAGGERED BOTH SIDES
BROOM FINISH
GRANULAR FILL
UNDISTURBED SUBGRADE
3500 PSI CONCRETE

REDWOOD DIVIDER
SCALE 1 1/2" = 1'-0"

Fig. 7.2 *Detail for using redwood to create a four-foot square grid pattern in a concrete patio.*

dividers and small sections (4 feet square or less) of concrete need not be reinforced. The easiest reinforcing to use is welded-wire reinforcing mesh which can be purchased from your lumber yard or steel supplier. It comes in rolls which can be laid flat and propped up in place above your base so it will set approximately 1-1/2 inches from the bottom of your paving. Most mesh used for residential work is 6 x 6 - W1.4 x W1.4.

The thickness of the concrete for your paving should not be less than 4 inches. For driveways to be capable of handling trucks and moving vans, 5 inches is recommended. Concrete expands and contracts with temperature changes as described in Chapter 4. Thus expansion and contraction joints must be installed to allow for this movement. Expansion joints should be 1/2 inch thickness and the full width and depth of the pavement. You can purchase from your lumber yard a pre-formed asphalt impregnated fiber board strip 4 inches wide which can be easily placed against a temporary 2 x 4 form as you pour your pavement. The next pour will go against the back side of this same 2 x 4 form completely, and then carefully removed leaving the 1/2 inch expansion strip behind by itself. For sidewalks, expansion joints should be placed every 30 feet; for driveways and other large paving surfaces, 20 feet. Permanent wood dividers can be installed in concrete paving which will serve as both expansion and contraction joints. Redwood, cedar, or pressure treated wood can be installed. In areas of freezing temperatures, be sure to install the nails driven into the dividers as illustrated to prevent them from heaving from frost. Contraction joints are joints which are tooled into the surface of the concrete after it is in place. You can purchase a double edging tool to do this job. Contraction joints should be placed anywhere there is a possibility of cracking occurring. In a 5-foot wide sidewalk, the best technique is to place the contraction joint every five feet thus creating a square which is aesthetically pleasing as well as functional. For drives, rectangles can be created in the placement of the joints, or in the case of large patios, squares, rectangles, or a combination of both.

The actual placement of concrete as it leaves the mixer or ready-mix truck includes screeding, vibrating, tamping, floating and edging.

Finishes. Concrete surfaces can be finished several ways. One method is to stop after using the wood float. The next technique is to use a coarse bristle broom and create a series of lines uniformly across the surface by pulling the broom across the freshly floated surface. This method provides a good coarse surface which helps prevent slipping when the pavement is wet. Other methods include either exposing the aggregates or stamping the surface with various patterns, but these are highly specialized tasks and will need to be done by an experienced and competent contractor. (Figures 7.1 to 7.4) If you would like to color your concrete as described in Chapter 4, you will need to purchase the pigment from a local masonry supply store and mix it in the concrete at the time you add the cement. If you purchase ready-mix you will need to contact the plant about the best method of adding color which is compatible with their system of operation. Please note that there is a possibility of color variation from one batch to the next. If you do not like the appearance of broom finish concrete, but like the idea of a rough surface you can purchase aluminum oxide grains and sprinkle them onto the final surface after floating and lightly trowel them into the surface with your wood float. For a sparkling finish spread silicon carbide grains (1/4 to 1/2 pound per square foot) over the entire surface and lightly trowel into place.

Fig. 7.3

Fig. 7.4

Fig. 7.3 - 7.4 *These are just a few of the patterns that can be created on the surface of concrete paving with the use of metal stamps.*

Fig. 7.5 *Ceramic tile walk through River Birch trees to the pool in the background. Design by Mark M. Holeman Inc.*

Brick

There are two ways of laying brick for paving. One is to mortar them over a concrete base or just laying them over a sand bed. For a permanent, high quality pavement, the concrete base method is the best. When using pavers which are less than 1-1/2 inches thick, it is the only recommended method. The concrete base should be the same as specified earlier for concrete paving. Mortar consists of 1 part portland cement, 1/2 part hydrated lime and 4-1/2 parts sand. Water is added to this mix until a thick paste is formed. A paste is too thin if it will not hold the weight of a brick by itself. Hand pressure is needed to push the brick into position until the correct thickness of the joint is achieved. The paste is too thick if you cannot easily push the brick into position. A bed of mortar approximately 3/4 inch is depth is placed over the concrete; the brick are laid on top in the desired pattern making sure each is level with the next and a uniform surface is created; then the spaces between the brick are filled with mortar and tooled with a section of electrical conduit to create a smooth concave joint as illustrated later in this chapter under the subject of brick walls.

When laying brick over a sand bed, 2 inches of sand can be laid over a firm soil base for patios and walks, but drives will need a gravel base as described for concrete pavement. Decomposed granite and crushed limestone with particles no larger than 1/4 inch and a large amount of fines can be used in place of sand and will be easier to use in localities where these materials are available. Pavers that are 1-1/2 inches or more in depth can be used for walks and patios, but 2 inches or more is recommended for drives. Dust and dirt will eventually creep into the joints of brick laid over sand and allow the germination of grass and week seeds. These can be held under control by using a pre-emergent herbicide. In shady areas moss may grow, which in some situations you might find attractive.

The use of high quality brick is very important in any area that is subject to freezing temperatures.

Fig. 7.6 *High quality worn and old brick can make an attractive patio. Design by A. E. Bye and Associates.*

The bricks must be dense and fired at a high temperature so that they are not capable of absorbing water. Brick which absorb water will soon break apart after several cycles of freezing and thawing. High quality brick may not be available in every section of the country. Contact your local masonry supply store. While brick may be available locally, the price may be prohibitive due to transportation costs. Preparing cost estimates for different types of paving may help you make the most economical comparisons. When stone is available locally, it may be less expensive to use as a pavement than brick that must be transported some distance. Some suppliers will have half brick available which will minimize cutting. You can cut brick with a 4-inch masonry chisel, but sometimes the brick will break at other locations than where you want and a few will be wasted. Some masonry supply stores have cutting service available using power masonry saws and will cut your brick for you for a small charge. This can be especially helpful when you are cutting angles or any other unusual shapes to fit existing conditions.

Drainage of brick surfaces is just as important as for any other paving surface. Follow the same directions for draining brick paving as discussed for concrete paving.

Patterns and Edgings. Several patterns can be created as you lay brick. The most common and easiest to lay is running bond which works especially well if the brick are not all of uniform size. If the brick are of a uniform size — 4 x 8 inches — use the basket weave or herringbone patterns. Other sizes and styles of brick are available in some areas of the country: small and large squares and hexagonal pavers. (Figures 7.7 to 7.11)

Fig. 7.8 - 7.10 Hexagonal, rectangular and square brick pavers.

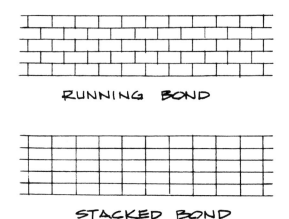

Fig. 7.7 Three patterns for brick paving.

Fig. 7.8

Fig. 7.10

Fig. 7.9

Fig. 7.11 *Rectangular and square brick pavers.*

Fig. 7.12 *Squares and rectangles of Bluestone laid over sand.*

Fig. 7.14 *Granite pavers.*

Most brick (and other materials) laid on sand need some sort of edging to prevent the brick sides from moving. The edging least noticeable is 1/4 or 3/16 thick by 4-inch high steel, which is available commercially. (Contact landscape contractors in your area to find your local supplier.) Other techniques involve laying bricks on end, pouring concrete edging in place against the brick paving or before placing the brick, or installing treated wood 2 x 4s. All of the edging except the wood 2 x 4s can be used for creating curves.

Stone

Stone can be laid in much the same manner as brick, although those types which come irregular in shape will require more labor and time to fit the joints. Like brick, some types of stone like soft sandstone and limestone can absorb moisture and break apart during freezing weather. Stone lends itself beautifully to landscaping uses because of its rustic appearance and the fact that it is a natural material. (Figures 7.12 to 7.14) Stone laid over sand should not be less than 1-1/2 inches thick. If you are laying stone over a concrete base it can be as thin as 3/4 inch. Slate is a very hard stone and usually comes quite thin and needs a concrete base to support it. The availability of stone at a reasonable price is dependent upon transportation costs. Buying that stone which is indigenous to the area you live in will be the least expensive. In large cities there are stores which specialize in stocking and selling stone. They can be found under the heading of 'stone' in the yellow pages or you can contact local masonry supply stores for stone sources as many will carry stone alongside brick.

Fig. 7.13 *Square stone pavers in fishscale pattern.*

Pre-cast Concrete Pavers

There are basically two types of pre-cast concrete pavers: one comes as large squares or rectangles which are most often used as stepping stones, the other is more like brick, but generally thicker. While almost the same size as brick they come in a variety of shapes which are interlocking in character and are ideal for drives and roads. (Figures 7.15 to 7.18) They are 2 inches or more thick and tolerate very heavy traffic. These latter pavers can be laid on 2 inches of sand for patios or over a sand and gravel base (or decomposed granite or crushed limestone) for drives as described for brick pavers. Contact masonry supply stores for the purchase of pre-cast pavers. Some of the irregular shapes may have to be ordered.

Fig. 7.15 *Pre-cast concrete pavers.*

Fig. 7.16 *Pre-cast concrete pavers.*

Fig. 7.17 *Pre-cast concrete pavers.*

Fig. 7.18 *Pre-cast concrete pavers surrounding a swimming pool. Landscape design by Barbara J. Ziolkowski.*

122

Fig. 7.19 *Square concrete pavers in a random pattern. Landscape design by Barbara J. Ziolkowski.*

Fig. 7.20 *Epoxy and pebbles as a veneer over a concrete base. Brown and light tan pebbles in a half-inch thickness provide color, contrast and a rich appearing finish to a home entrance.*

Wood

Wood that has been preserved is quite useful as a paving material if it is not used where there is a lot of activity with bare feet. Wood treated with creosote (railroad ties) or pentachlorophenol should not be used. Use new wood treated with one of the metallic salts such as chromated copper arsenate. Sections of 6 x 6 inch timber can be cut 4 to 6 inches thick and laid over 2 inches of sand in the same manner as brick pavers. Not all lumber yards may carry treated wood so inquiries may need to be made to several to find it. It will cost more than untreated wood, but will be much less expensive than redwood or cedar.

EDGINGS

Edgings help define the lines of the design used for paving and other areas of the landscape. They can make maintenance easier because they provide a physical separation between grass and the mulching of a planting bed. Edgings also inhibit the growth of grass into the bed, and if the edges are a few inches wide, they act as a mowing strip, permitting the wheel of the mower to ride along on top of the edging material. Finally edgings provide increased stability to the edges of materials like asphalt or brick on sand and ensure that the edges will be neat and uniform.

Concrete is an ideal edging material because it can be poured into any shape or form. (Figures 7.22 to 7.23) Brick and stone can be used as veneers over concrete. Metals are frequently used as edgings; some stores carry an expensive corrugated aluminum edging, but this is usually so thin and soft that it crushes easily and is not recommended. Steel 1/8 inch thick, 4 inches high and in 16-foot lengths is a good edging material. (Figures 7.21 and 7.24) Aluminum strips in 1/8 and 3/16 inch thicknesses and in the same height as steel are available. The anodized type is highly recommended. The sections come as straight pieces but can be bent to make curves or cut and welded for 90-degree corners. Contact landscape contractors in your area for the source of supply. They will be more likely to carry this product than a steel supplier who handles reinforcing rods and similar steel products.

There are several plastic edging products on the market, but the type which seem to work best has a loop on the top edge and a hook on the bottom to which a stake is attached. It can be bent to fit any desired curve or cut and butted for 90-degree corners. It is less expensive and easier to install than steel. Contact local nurseries and landscape contractors to secure this product.

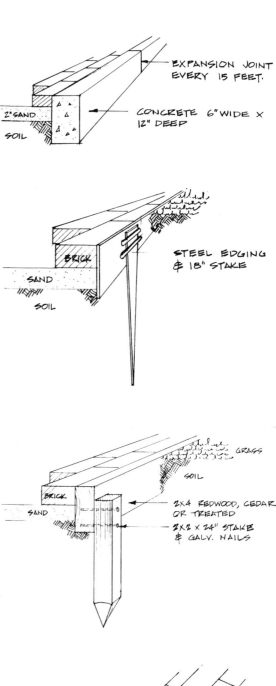

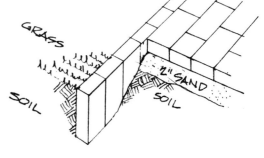

Fig. 7.21 *Details of various types of edging.*

Fig. 7.22 *Concrete edging.*

Fig. 7.23 *Concrete edging with a layer of brick mortared on top.*

Fig. 7.24 *Steel edging. See Fig. 7.21 for installation detail.*

Wood is another good edging material. The most popular wood edging consists of 2 x 4s laid in straight lines. Because any wood edging will be in contact with the soil, it must have natural decay resistant properties; use redwood, cedar, or wood treated with a waterborne salt like chromated copper arsenate. For gentle curves, use single 1/2 x 4-inch strips of redwood; laminate the strips for wider edging. (Figures 7.25 to 7.27) For a heavy edging use old railroad ties, or lay new, treated 4 x 4s or 6 x 6s flush with the surface of the ground. Hold heavy edgings in place by drilling holes in the wood and driving pipe or steel reinforcing rods through the holes. The holes and steel can be as small as 1/2 inch in diameter.

The wood, plastic, and steel edgings can be installed simply by cutting a narrow trench in the soil no deeper than the height of the edging; lay the edging in the trench; stake into place, replace the soil on both sides and tamp. The installation of a concrete edge is a little more complicated because forming is required. When forming curves use thin plywood or sheet steel. Curves require frequent staking to rigidly hold the forms into place. To ensure that the width of the concrete remains constant you may want to leave your stakes 2 inches above the forms and tie them together tightly with wire. If your stakes are wood 2 x 2s you can use a 1 x 2 nailed onto the stop of each to maintain the correct space.

Some of these edgings are subject to heaving in freeze-thaw climates; tamp down the edging in the spring if it rises above the adjacent surfaces.

Fig. 7.25 *Timber edging using a 4 x 6.*

Fig. 7.26 *Round timber edging.*

Fig. 7.27 *Two half-inch strips of redwood bent and fastened together to form a curved edging.*

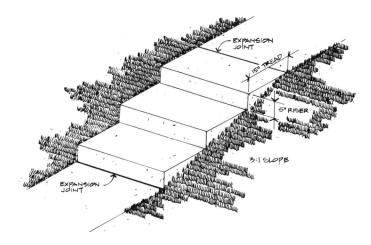

Fig. 7.28 *Steps (5" riser and 15" tread) to fit a 3:1 slope which can be grass.*

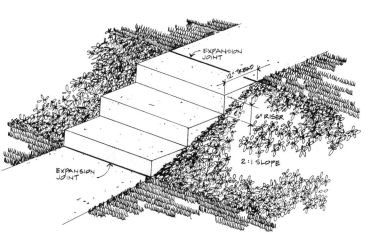

Fig. 7.29 *Steps (6" riser and 12" tread) to fit a 2:1 slope (ground cover or shrubs).*

STEPS

To get from one horizontal plane to a higher or lower horizontal plane on your site, put in steps. Install ramps or long slopes if any handicapped people, including those in wheelchairs, must traverse the area. Steps can be made of concrete, brick and stone veneers over concrete, or wood timbers.

Steps should be at least 4 feet wide. The number of steps needed to achieve a vertical rise is determined by the vertical distance between two horizontal planes; generally use a minimum of three steps in any one grouping. A single step is quite hazardous because it is very difficult to see, especially for people with limited vision. Use no more than 19 steps in any single group; eleven steps are optimum. Use landings no less than 4 feet long to break up groups of steps. Overall you can use any odd number of steps to fit any type of slope.

There are many formulas for figuring riser (height of steps) -tread (depth of steps) ratios. But in some instances the formulas result in awkwardly placed steps if they are not used correctly. For our purposes in this book, there are three useful riser-tread relationships. (1) The maximum ratio results from a 6-inch riser and a 12-inch tread (2:1); this fits a planted slope and is the steepest for outdoor use. (2) A less steep rise is 5-1/2 inches high with a 14-inch tread. This rise is easy to construct with 2 x 6 lumber (which is usually 5-1/2 inches wide). (3) A 5-inch rise and a 15-inch tread (3:1) fits a slope on which grass can be grown; however, it may be somewhat difficult for short-legged people to climb.

Fig. 7.31 *Concrete steps with exposed aggregate treads. Design by Doede, Inc.*

Fig. 7.30 *Concrete steps offset to create a meandering pattern through the garden.*

Concrete

Concrete steps are constructed by excavating the soil on the slope to a depth which will allow the placement of a compacted gravel base of at least 5 inches as described in the concrete paving section earlier in this chapter. About 1-1/2 inches above the base, place a grid system of 1/2 inch diameter reinforcing rods propped up with rocks or broken brick to hold it in place. The forms are then put in place using 2-inch thick lumber for the risers (2 x 6 for a 5-1/2 inch rise, or 2 x 8 ripped down to 6 inches for a 6-inch rise). The thickness of the concrete used for steps depends on the width of the steps. As a general rule for 4-inch wide steps the depth of the concrete should be 4 inches from the base of the riser to a line perpendicular with the top of the gravel base; a 5-inch depth is suitable for 5 to 6 foot wide steps, and a 6-inch depth is for steps more than 6 feet wide. Plywood (5/8 inch or thicker) can be used for the sides of the steps with the riser forms nailed to it. All of the forms need to be staked and braced to keep them in position. If your steps are more than 4 feet wide place a brace down the center nailed to each riser form and stake it at the bottom to keep the center of the steps from bowing outward.

Finish the treads of all concrete steps with a rough texture to prevent people from slipping in wet weather. This can be done with a wood float (as described in the concrete paving section), or by adding aluminum oxide grains during the final finishing. Also slope the treads slightly for drainage (1/8 inch/foot is recommended). Stone rub the riser to match the float finish of the treads. This can be done by using a Carborundum stone (looks like a stone block with a trowel handle attached) with a paste of cement, sand, and water, applied and rubbed right after the forms are removed. An edger should be used along the top of the riser during the finishing process to reduce the sharpness of this upper edge of the steps.

If the top and bottom of your steps will be ultimately joined with concrete walks, be sure to place a 1/2 inch expansion joint in both places. If you have a lot of steps, put in at least one handrail on a side. The height of the handrail above the nose of the steps should be about 32 inches. If the steps will be used at night install some lighting (covered later in this chapter).

If you would like to have some brick or stone steps as part of your landscape to match those same materials used elsewhere such as for walks and patios, you simply construct a set of concrete steps as described earlier and use a veneer of brick or stone. (Figures 7.32 to 7.35) The steps will need to

Fig. 7.32 *Concrete steps with brick and stone veneer. Design by Claire Bennett.*

Fig. 7.33 *Stone veneer steps. Design by Browning Day Mullins Dierdorf, Inc.*

Fig. 7.34 *Stone and rock steps.*

be built down lower to allow for the thickness of the brick or stone and a 3/4 inch thick mortar setting bed. The placement of these veneer materials is the same as for paving described earlier in this chapter.

Wood

Six-inch timbers are excellent for steps because their true dimension is 5-1/2 inches, which is an ideal height. (Fig. 7.37) Hold timbers in place by drilling vertical holes in them and driving into the holes 30- to 36-inch reinforcing bars 1/2 inch in diameter; use two bars for each step. Additional timbers can be installed for treads or gravel and shredded hardwood bark mulches can be used, depending upon the appearance desired and the amount of traffic that will be on the steps. The mulches will be kicked away gradually under heavy foot traffic. (Fig. 7.39)

Fig. 7.35 *Brick veneer steps. Design by McConaghie/Batt and Associates.*

Fig. 7.36 *Wood steps and timber retaining wall are a harmonious combination. Landscape design by Barbara J. Ziolkowski.*

Fig. 7.37 *Steps built with 6 x 6 treated timbers. Design by Walker Harris Associates, Inc.*

Fig. 7.38 *Wood steps to match deck. Design by Theodore Brickman Co.*

Fig. 7.39 *Timber and gravel steps with rock to hold the side slopes. Design by Theodore Brickman Co.*

FREE-STANDING WALLS

This type of wall is much like a fence in contrast to a retaining wall which other has its downhill side exposed to view. It can be constructed of brick, stone, in-situ concrete, concrete block, precast concrete decorative units, or a combination of all of these. Most of our discussion here will be about brick walls but the principles and techniques will also apply to the other materials as well. Because any material used in the construction of a wall is fully exposed to the weather, it should be of high quality and freeze-thaw resistant. Brick must be severe weather (SW) rated and hard-fired, with low moisture absorbency. The other materials — stone, concrete block, pre-cast concrete — also must be capable of resisting moisture absorption. Footings (the base of the wall below ground) for brick walls will be concrete with some reinforcement. The exact size of the footing and the amount of reinforcement depends upon soil conditions, but generally the size of the footing should not be less than 10 inches deep by 16 inches wide, with two 3/8 inch reinforcing bars continuous from one end of the footing to the other. Footings should be as deep or deeper than the frost line (see frost depth map in Appendix B), or as necessary to counteract wind forces. Usually this is 3 feet or more. Footings for low walls (3 feet or less) in frost-free areas can be placed less than 3 feet deep. The foundation (portion of wall below ground but on top of footing) can be concrete block rather than poured-in place concrete which will reduce the amount of labor required for forming and save you the cost of buying concrete. If brick are not too expensive, it might be more practical to lay the brick directly on top of a footing rather than construct a foundation. If using concrete block or preparing price comparisons between brick and block, keep in mind that 3 courses of brick are 8 inches high which is equal to one course of concrete block.

Vertical reinforcing is needed in areas of high winds. The Brick Institute recommends that for 10 pounds per square foot wind pressure a straight wall should not be higher than three-fourths of the wall thickness squared. (See Table 7.1) For example, this is 3 feet for an 8-inch wall. Reinforced concrete piers extending from the top of the wall to 3 to 4 feet below grade with a brick veneer to match the wall can be used to compensate for wind pressure. Instead of piers you can construct buttresses or use a series of offsets to strengthen the wall. (Figures 7.43 to 7.44) Serpentine walls are attractive and self-reinforcing if built according to this formula: For a 4-inch thick wall, the radius of curvature should be no more than twice the height of the wall above the ground line and the depth of curvature no less than one-half the height. (Fig. 7.53) Such walls are difficult

Fig. 7.40 *In-situ concrete wall.*

Fig. 7.41 *Wall of square blocks of granite.*

131

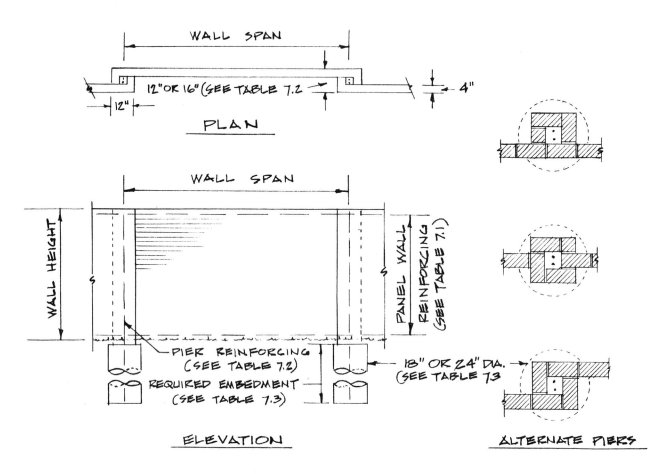

Fig. 7.42 *Pier and panel garden wall.*

TABLE 7.1 Panel Wall Reinforcing Steel

Wall Span, ft	Vertical Spacing, in.								
	Wind Load, 10 psf			Wind Load, 15 psf			Wind Load, 20 psf		
	A	B	C	A	B	C	A	B	C
8	45	30	19	30	20	12	23	15	9.5
10	29	19	12	19	13	8.0	14	10	6.0
12	20	13	8.5	13	9.0	5.5	10	7.0	4.0
14	15	10	6.5	10	6.5	4.0	7.5	5.0	3.0
16	11	7.5	5.0	7.5	5.0	3.0	6.0	4.0	2.5

Note: A = 2 - no. 2 bars
B = 2 - 3/16-in. diam wires
C = 2 - 9-gage wires

TABLE 7.2 Pier Reinforcing Steel

Wall Span, ft	Wind Load, 10 psf			Wind Load, 15 psf			Wind Load, 20 psf		
	Wall Height, ft			Wall Height, ft			Wall Height, ft		
	4	6	8	4	6	8	4	6	8
8	2#3	2#4	2#5	2#3	2#5	2#6	2#4	2#5	2#5
10	2#3	2#4	2#5	2#4	2#5	2#7	2#4	2#6	2#6
12	2#3	2#5	2#6	2#4	2#6	2#6	2#4	2#6	2#7
14	2#3	2#5	2#6	2#4	2#6	2#6	2#5	2#5	2#7
16	2#4	2#5	2#7	2#4	2#6	2#7	2#5	2#6	2#7

(a) Within heavy lines 12 × 16-in. pier required. All other values obtained with 12 × 12-in. pier.

TABLE 7.3 Required Embedment for Pier Foundation

Wall Span, ft	Wind Load, 10 psf			Wind Load, 15 psf			Wind Load, 20 psf		
	Wall Height, ft			Wall Height, ft			Wall Height, ft		
	4	6	8	4	6	8	4	6	8
8	2'-0"	2'-3"	2'-9"	2'-3"	2'-6"	3'-0"	2'-3"	2'-9"	3'-0"
10	2'-0"	2'-6"	2'-9"	2'-3"	2'-9"	3'-3"	2'-6"	3'-0"	3'-3"
12	2'-3"	2'-6"	3'-0"	2'-3"	3'-0"	3'-3"	2'-6"	3'-3"	3'-6"
14	2'-3"	2'-9"	3'-0"	2'-6"	3'-0"	3'-3"	2'-9"	3'-3"	3'-9"
16	2'-3"	2'-9"	3'-0"	2'-6"	3'-3"	3'-6"	2'-9"	3'-3"	4'-0"

(a) Within heavy lines 24-in. diam. foundation required. All other values obtained with 18-in. diam. foundation.

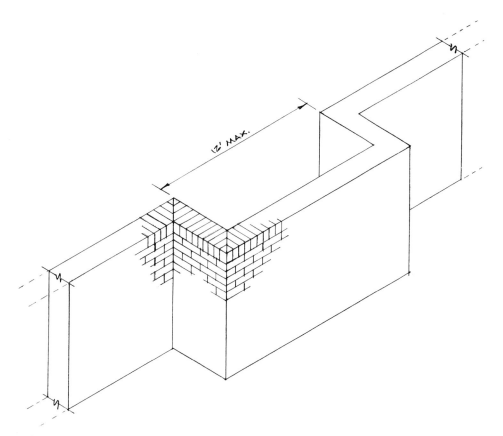

Fig. 7.43 *Two-foot offsets can be used to increase a wall's resistance to wind damage.*

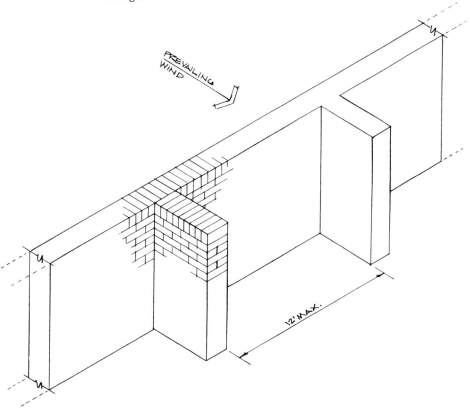

Fig. 7.44 *Buttresses can be used to strengthen a brick wall.*

to build and construction of them should be placed in the hands of a competent contractor. Running bond is the most commonly used pattern for laying bricks. Other patterns include stacked, English, and Flemish bonds. These can also be varied by recessing the brick or projecting it outward to create shadows or by combining it with other materials such as tile or decorative concrete block. All walls need some sort of coping or cap. Lay brick in a rowlock pattern on top, or lay natural stone or pre-cast concrete. (Figures 7.50 to 7.51)

The quality of mortar is important because it is the weakest part of the wall. Use Type S mortar which is 1 part portland cement, 1/2 part hydrated lime, and 4-1/2 parts sand. Water is added until you obtain a thick paste. A paste which is too thin will not hold the brick up in position for the right thickness of joint in the wall. A paste which is too thick will make it difficult to push the brick down into position and the joint may be too large. Liquid latex can be used in place of water where increased resistance to frost damage is desired.

Joints typically vary from 1/4 to 1/2 inch in size. Your walls will look best when the joints are as uniform as you can possibly make them. (Fig. 7.52) There are several ways you can seal the surface of the joint after you have laid the brick. The two best surfaces which provide the best seal against moisture penetration, and frost damage are the concave and v-shaped.

Vertical expansion joints are needed for long walls to relieve the stress of expansion and contraction, and minimize the possibility of cracking and failure of the wall. Place the joints every 50 feet. If you would like to add wood trim, fixtures, or brackets to hold espaliered trees in place, the ideal time to do this is during the construction of the wall. Metal plugs with or without fiber inserts, or expansion shields can be placed in the joints during construction. You can obtain these items from a hardware store. Should you forget to install them, you will need to drill holes in the joints with a carbide tipped drill and insert the expansion shield. Some of the new adhesives such as urethane can be used to glue items directly to the wall.

Many masonry walls are affected by the deposit of water-soluable salts on their outside surfaces; this deposit is called efflorescence, which is usually white and ugly. High-quality brick and mortar minimizes the occurrence of efflorescence, but if the deposit occurs, clean it with a solution of muriatic acid, which is sold at hardware stores.

Fig. 7.45 *Brick wall with pillars.*

Fig. 7.46 *A brick wall painted to match the house.*

Fig. 7.47 *Four-inch tile allow air passage through this brick wall. Plants obscure the pillars.*

Fig. 7.48 *'Z' shaped wall.*

Fig. 7.49 *Spacing bricks approximately 2-1/2" allows air passage and adds shadow patterns.*

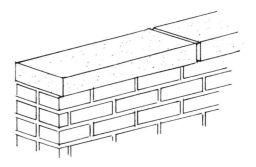

Fig. 7.50 *Stone or pre-cast concrete caps for brick walls.*

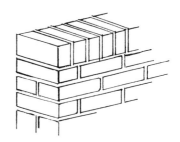

Fig. 7.51 *Rowlock pattern for a brick cap.*

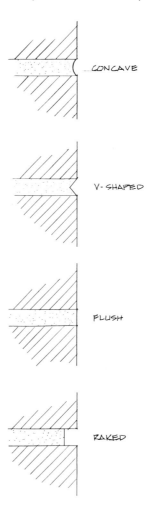

CONCAVE

V-SHAPED

FLUSH

RAKED

Fig. 7.52 *Four types of mortar joints.*

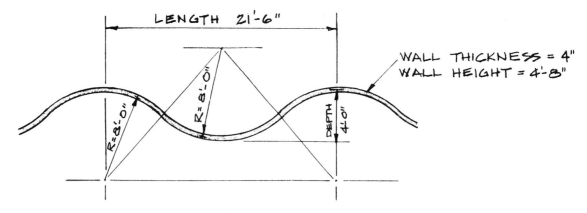

Fig. 7.53 *Plan for a serpentine wall.*

Fig. 7.54 *Serpentine brick wall.*

Fig. 7.55 *Stone wall.*

Fig. 7.56 *Stone wall.*

Fig. 7.57 *Pre-cast concrete block wall.*

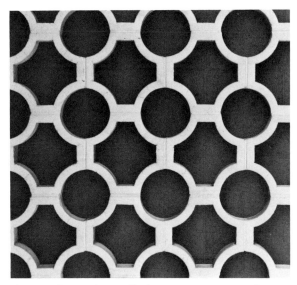

Fig. 7.58 *Decorative wall of pre-cast concrete units.*

Fig. 7.59 *Pre-cast concrete decorative blocks.*

Fig. 7.60 *Pre-cast concrete decorative blocks.*

RETAINING WALLS

If you have a small, sloping land area and need to have as much flat space as possible, retaining walls are desirable. A vertical retaining wall consumes the least amount of horizontal space, but if you can spare a little sloping, dry stone walls, gravity type walls, or timbers can be used to hold the soil in place. Concrete retaining walls can be reinforced cantilever walls (L shape or invert T shape), or gravity walls which will be stable because of their monolithic mass. For low retaining walls the accompanying chart will give you the size and dimensions of the concrete and reinforcing.

If you need a wall which is higher than illustrated in the charts, or if your ground will continue to slope up behind the top of the wall after it is built, you should contact a professional consultant for assistance (see Appendix A).

The base or bottom of the footing of all retaining walls should rest on the original soil of the site, or soil which has been undisturbed by construction activity. If you excavate into disturbed soil which will likely be fill, you will need to continue to excavate until you reach original soil. Such soil is usually very firm and consistent in color. Most walls will be subject to a lot of hydraulic pressure on their backsides caused by the horizontal movement of water downhill. If the pressure is not relieved, it will cause the wall to fail. One of the simplest ways of providing drainage is to place small weep holes (2 inches in diameter — PVC plastic pipe is ideal) in the wall just above the lower level soil surface. Water on the backside of the wall will creep through the holes. Put a pocket of gravel behind the weep holes to help accumulate the water and allow it to pass through. If you happen to forget to install weep holes, before pouring the concrete, it is possible to drill holes through the wall with a masonry bit and large portable electric drill. Drilling is the best method for creating weep holes in timber retaining walls. No weep holes will be needed for dry stone walls as there will be sufficient cracks available for the water to escape. You will need weep holes, however, if you decide to use mortar between the stones. To prevent any moisture from seeping through the concrete in places other than weep holes, apply a coat of asphalt emulsion to the backside of the wall, add a sheet of polyethylene and another coat of asphalt. Contractors use a similar technique for sealing basement walls under homes.

Concrete retaining walls can be attractive if you use a good finishing technique, such as shadow lines. One technique is to use various thicknesses of rough wood inside the forms before the concrete is poured. (Fig. 7.61) The wood layers will create shadow lines and also provide a rough texture, and the grain or knot patterns will add interest. Good finishing enables the walls to blend harmoniously into the landscape. Rubber mats of various types, sizes, and shapes inside the forms also add many kinds of patterns and textures to the concrete surface. (Figures 7.65 to 7.66) By providing a lip at the lower level of a retaining wall it is possible to veneer the exposed face of the concrete with brick, stone, or pre-cast concrete. The veneer is attached to the concrete by using galvanized masonry ties (strips of metal about 1 inch wide by 6 inches long) which are nailed to the concrete and bent over into the mortar joint. When installed every 2 to 3 feet horizontally and vertically, they help securely tie the veneer to the wall.

Fig. 7.61 *Rough sawn wood placed in forms creates an interesting pattern of shadows and textures.*

Fig. 7.62 *Terraced concrete retaining wall.*

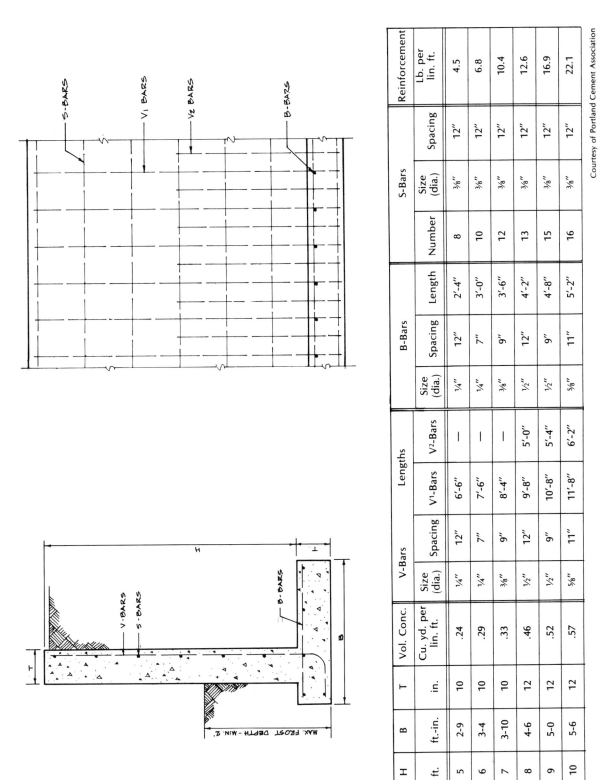

Fig. 7.63 *Cantilever retaining walls without surcharge.*

H	B	T	Vol. Conc.	V-Bars		Lengths		B-Bars				S-Bars			Reinforcement
				Size (dia.)	Spacing	V¹-Bars	V²-Bars	Size (dia.)	Spacing	Length	Number	Size (dia.)	Spacing		
ft.	ft.-in.	in.	Cu. yd. per lin. ft.												Lb. per lin. ft.
5	2-9	10	.24	¼″	12″	6'-6″	—	¼″	12″	2'-4″	8	⅜″	12″		4.5
6	3-4	10	.29	¼″	7″	7'-6″	—	¼″	7″	3'-0″	10	⅜″	12″		6.8
7	3-10	10	.33	⅜″	9″	8'-4″	—	⅜″	9″	3'-6″	12	⅜″	12″		10.4
8	4-6	12	.46	½″	12″	9'-8″	5'-0″	½″	12″	4'-2″	13	⅜″	12″		12.6
9	5-0	12	.52	½″	9″	10'-8″	5'-4″	½″	9″	4'-8″	15	⅜″	12″		16.9
10	5-6	12	.57	⅝″	11″	11'-8″	6'-2″	⅝″	11″	5'-2″	16	⅜″	12″		22.1

Courtesy of Portland Cement Association

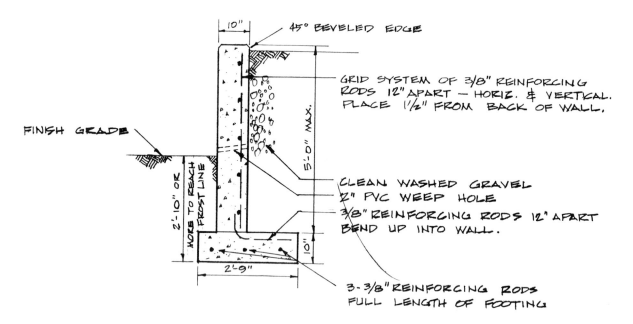

10"

45° BEVELED EDGE

GRID SYSTEM OF 3/8" REINFORCING
RODS 12" APART — HORIZ. & VERTICAL.
PLACE 1½" FROM BACK OF WALL.

FINISH GRADE

5'-0" MAX.

2'-10" OR MORE TO REACH FROST LINE

CLEAN WASHED GRAVEL
2" PVC WEEP HOLE
3/8" REINFORCING RODS 12" APART
BEND UP INTO WALL.

10"

2'-9"

3 - 3/8" REINFORCING RODS
FULL LENGTH OF FOOTING

Fig. 7.64 *Detail for a concrete retaining wall based upon the information given in Fig. 7.56.*

Fig. 7.65 *Surface texture created by leaving spaces between form boards.*

Fig. 7.66 *After the special forms are removed, the projections are removed with a hammer to create the coarse texture.*

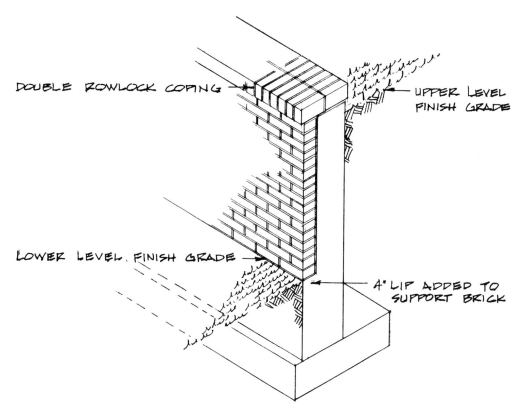

DOUBLE ROWLOCK COPING

UPPER LEVEL FINISH GRADE

LOWER LEVEL FINISH GRADE

4" LIP ADDED TO SUPPORT BRICK

Fig. 7.67 *Detail for a concrete retaining wall with brick veneer. Stone and other veneers can be used in the same manner.*

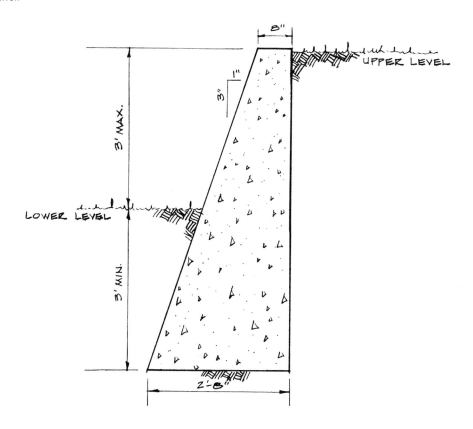

8"

1"

3"

3' MAX.

3' MIN.

UPPER LEVEL

LOWER LEVEL

2'-8"

Fig. 7.68 *Detail for a gravity-type concrete retaining wall.*

All concrete retaining walls will need to be reinforced with steel bars. The size and spacing is listed in the charts shown earlier.

Long retaining walls need vertical expansion and contraction joints. Expansion joints can be much like those described in the concrete paving section earlier in this chapter. Reinforcing rods do not go through the joint; they must stop on each side preferably 1-1/2 inches from the joint. Contraction joints are easiest to provide by cutting a 1-1/2 inch triangle from the 2 x 4 and place it vertically against the form facing the lower side or outside face of the retaining walls. You will get a v-shaped vertical groove 1/2 inches deep and the wall will likely crack there if it has to. Install expansion joints every 100 feet and contraction joints every 25 feet, though they might be as close as 10 feet apart.

Fig. 7.69 *Strong shadow patterns result when the joints are recessed.*

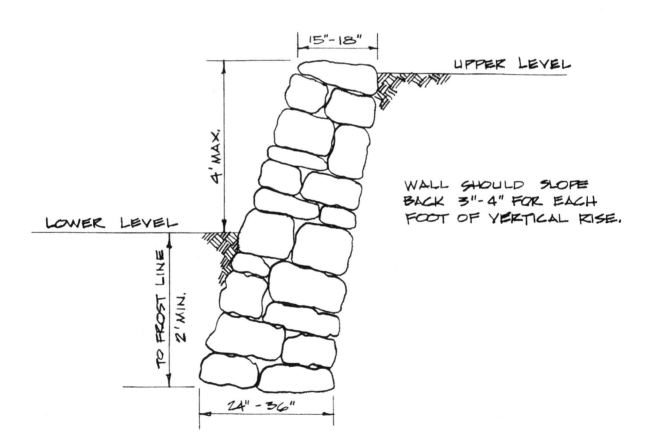

Fig. 7.70 *Detail for a stone wall.*

142

Fig. 7.71 *Random size rock.*

Fig. 7.72 *Volcanic rock.*

Fig. 7.73 *Sloping concrete retaining wall with field stone veneer.*

Fig. 7.74 *Large rock can retain a slope and with topsoil in pockets, low growing plants can be established to 'soften' the hard appearance of the rock. Design by A. E. Bye and Associates.*

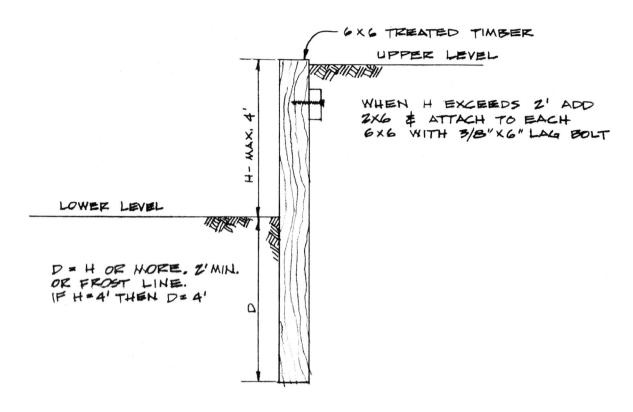

6×6 TREATED TIMBER

UPPER LEVEL

WHEN H EXCEEDS 2' ADD
2×6 & ATTACH TO EACH
6×6 WITH 3/8"×6" LAG BOLT

H-MAX. 4'

LOWER LEVEL

D = H OR MORE, 2' MIN.
OR FROST LINE.
IF H = 4' THEN D = 4'

D

Fig. 7.75 *Detail for a vertical timber retaining wall.*

Fig. 7.76 *Vertical timber retaining wall.*

Fig. 7.77 *Vertical timber retaining wall with buttresses.*

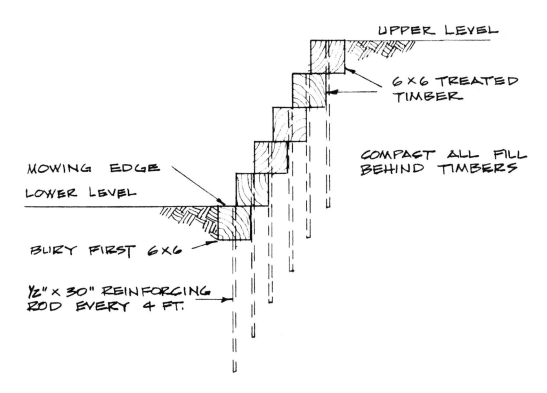

UPPER LEVEL

6 X 6 TREATED
TIMBER

COMPACT ALL FILL
BEHIND TIMBERS

MOWING EDGE
LOWER LEVEL

BURY FIRST 6X6

½" X 30" REINFORCING
ROD EVERY 4 FT.

Fig. 7.78 *Detail for a stepped timber retaining wall.*

Fig. 7.79 *Low wood retaining wall with wide top for seating.*

Fig. 7.80 *Wood fence screens the parking area. Design by Lloyd Bond.*

Fig. 7.81 *Shadow patterns from raised pieces on this wood fence.*

FENCES

Fences provide privacy, especially when they are built of solid materials and are 6 feet or more high. They also discourage trespassing, control human and animal traffic, identify property lines, define and emphasize entrances, and create and define outdoor space. You can create many styles and designs from wood, wrought iron, chainlink, and pipe. Wrought iron is highly ornamental and has some contemporary applications. Chainlink is commonly used, but is usually incompatible with the landscape. Most chainlink consists of woven wire fabric made of 9 or 11 gauge galvanized steel wire; galvanized steel pipes are used for the posts and rails. Some manufacturers now offer colored vinyl coatings that harmonize a little better with the landscape. Redwood slats can be inserted into the small loops formed by the wire fabric to provide a little more privacy. Chainlink fences are useful and the least expensive method for enclosing tennis courts and other recreational facilities. On hilly sites chainlink and split rail fences can follow the natural slopes. Other styles of fences will need to be stepped down. In some areas you may be required to erect a fence if you have a swimming pool, or similar 'attractive nuisance.' The most economical way to finance a fence is to secure the cooperation of your neighbors and share the cost. In that case the fence can be placed directly on the property line. Lacking this cooperation you should consider placing the fence inside your property line 6 inches to establish sole control.

Wood is a natural fencing material that harmonizes with most sites, and there are many creative ways it can be used in fence design. (Figures 7.80 to 7.103) The design of the fence will be dictated by its functional use as physical or a visual barrier. A height of 4 feet is enough for a physical barrier while 6 feet above level ground provides visual privacy. You will also need to consider whether the fence needs to allow air through it or be airtight. Air movement helps cool; openings relieved some of the pressure from high winds and help prevent the collapse of the fence. You can also construct a fence with buttresses or offsets, as described in the section on brick walls to increase wind resistance. Finally, the fence can be highly decorative — a work of art in itself — or just a simple structure acting as a backdrop for plantings or other features. Items that form a fence are posts, rails, boards, and fasteners. It is always cheaper to use standard lumber sizes; a lot of fitting and cutting to custom sizes increase the cost of the fence. Contract your local lumberyard to determine their stock fence materials. Other sizes will have to be ordered.

Posts are usually redwood, cedar or treated softwood 8 foot long 4 x 4s, although for short fences 12 foot long posts cut in half can be used. For short fences (less than 6 feet high) that allow air to pass through them, bury posts 2 to 2-1/2 feet below the finish grade; use 3 foot depth for 6 foot high fences and an even greater depth for higher fences. You can set posts in holes in the ground and tamp down the soil around them. But if the soil is soft or becomes soft after spring thaws, or in areas where high winds occur, you will have to surround the posts with concrete. For solid fences 6 feet high dig 12-inch diameter holes, insert the post, and completely surround the posts with concrete to the full depth of the holes. This provides sufficient wind residence except for tornadoes and hurricanes. Besides setting posts into holes, posts can also be set on top of concrete walls or 12-inch diameter concrete columns by setting steel angles or double metal straps into the concrete and then bolting the posts to the angles or straps.

If the fence rails are going to be laid flat rather than on edge, space posts no farther than 6 feet apart; this will reduce the possibility of the rails sagging. The posts can be spaced 8 feet apart when the rails are placed on edge. Rather than butting the rail to the post and toenailing, it is better to dado the post and insert the railing into the notch, or place the rail on the side of the post and nail directly into the post. Butting and toenailing do not provide sufficient strength and structural integrity. All nails and fasteners should be galvanized or otherwise corrosion resistant.

The boards that are attached to the rails can be of any width and character, but a range of 4 to 12 inches in width is the best (6- and 8-inch wide boards are the ones most commonly used). Pickets, grape stakes, are also effective when nailed to rails. Two rails are generally adequate for short fences, whereas three rails should be used for fences 6 feet or higher, to prevent the boards from warping and moving. A gate should be designed to harmonize with the fence. Structurally, the gate will have a square or rectangular frame, with a diagonal brace running from the top of the frame on the latch side down to the opposite side near the hinges. Such hardware as hinges and latches should be sturdy and weather and corrosion resistant. It may take a visit to several hardware stores and lumber yards to find what you want as few stores carry a very large selection. The post to which the gate is attached may have to be larger or deeper to make it sturdy enough to handle the extra strain. Redwood or cedar fences will weather to their natural gray color, or the wood can be stained or painted. When selecting redwood or cedar for posts, be sure to select heartwood (deep

red color) rather than the sapwood (creamy color) which is more subject to decay when it is in contact with the soil. Other types of wood will need to be stained or painted regularly unless they have been pressure treated with a preservative such as pentachlorophenol or chromated copper arsenate. In most instances painting or staining will increase long-term maintenance costs, but if not properly maintained, fences will look ugly as the paint or stain begins to wear off.

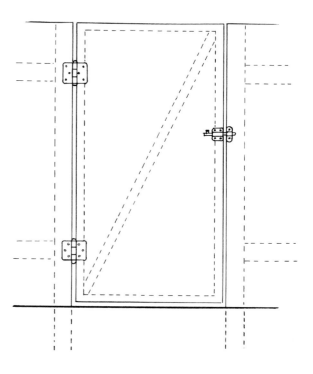

Fig. 7.82 *Detail of a wood gate which shows correct placement of cross brace to keep the gate from sagging.*

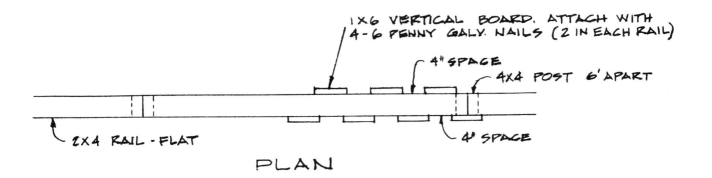

1X6 VERTICAL BOARD. ATTACH WITH
4-6 PENNY GALV. NAILS (2 IN EACH RAIL)

4" SPACE

4X4 POST 6' APART

4" SPACE

2X4 RAIL - FLAT

PLAN

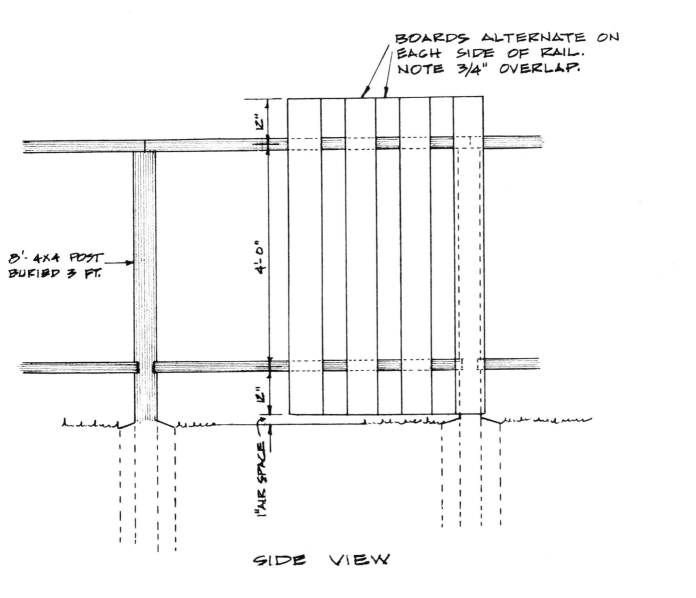

BOARDS ALTERNATE ON
EACH SIDE OF RAIL.
NOTE 3/4" OVERLAP.

12"

4'-0"

8'- 4X4 POST
BURIED 3 FT.

12"

1" AIR SPACE

SIDE VIEW

Fig. 7.83 Details for a simple wood fence which provides
both privacy and the passage of air.

149

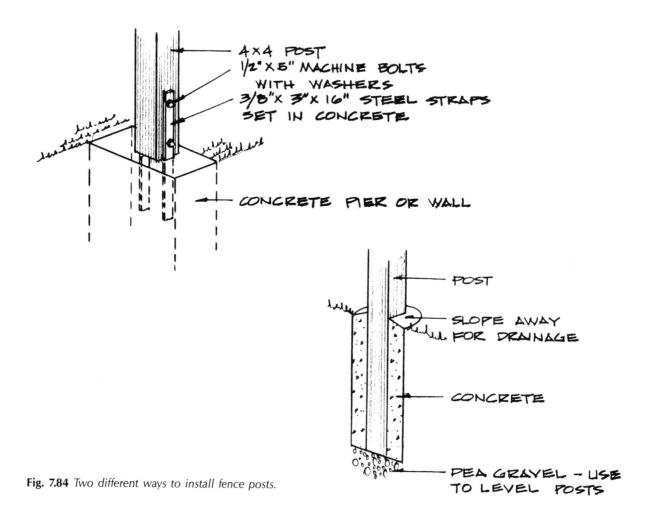

4×4 POST
1/2" × 5" MACHINE BOLTS
  WITH WASHERS
3/8" × 3" × 16" STEEL STRAPS
SET IN CONCRETE

CONCRETE PIER OR WALL

POST

SLOPE AWAY
FOR DRAINAGE

CONCRETE

PEA GRAVEL - USE
TO LEVEL POSTS

Fig. 7.84 *Two different ways to install fence posts.*

Fig. 7.85 *Cedar grape stake fence.*

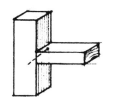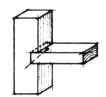

BUTT & TOENAIL (LEAST DESIRABLE) DADO (1/2" ± NOTCH CUT INTO POST - BETTER METHOD)

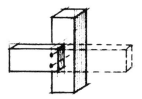

RAILS FLAT AGAINST POST JOINT IN CENTER OF POST

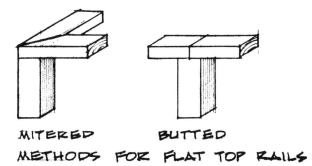

MITERED   BUTTED
METHODS FOR FLAT TOP RAILS

Fig. 7.86 *Details for attaching rails to posts.*

Fig. 7.87 *Contrast of dark and light vertical members.*

Fig. 7.88 *Each wood piece is a different size creating many varying shadow patterns.*

Fig. 7.89 *Design by James and Bonnie Bartell.*

Fig. 7.90 *Design by Paul Hayden Kirk.*

Fig. 7.91 *Design by LLoyd Bond.*

Fig. 7.92 *Design by A. O. Bumgardner.*

Fig. 7.89 - 7.96 *Fences can be a work of art.*

Fig. 7.93 *Design by John Vogley.*

Fig. 7.94 *Design by Robert Cornwall.*

154

Fig. 7.95 *Design by Lloyd Bond.*

Fig. 7.96 *Design by Doede, Inc.*

Fig. 7.97 *Design by Kirk, Wallace & McKinley.*

Fig. 7.98 *Backside of fence in Fig. 7.97.*

Fig. 7.99 *Design by Theodore Brickman Co.*

Fig. 7.102

Fig. 7.100

Fig. 7.103 *Design by Frits Loonsten.*

Fig. 7.101

Figures 7.97 - 7.103 *More creative ways to design wood fences.*

DECKS

Decks are ideal for extending or adding additional space at the same level as the floor of a home or for adding additional space on hillsides. Decks are especially popular for children because the space dries quickly after a storm, enabling the children to play long before other space, such as lawn areas, is sufficiently dry. You can add shelters or other overhead types of structure to decks to provide full or partial shade. The size and shape of the structure will be influenced by your needs and such characteristics as the direction of prevailing winds, the deck's orientation to the sun, and the topography of the site. If you are contemplating building the deck yourself, and have not had a lot of construction experience, you should keep it a simple square or rectangle. If it needs to be some other shape in order to fit your particular complex site, hiring a professional consultant such as a landscape architect is recommended (see Appendix A). This is especially true if you live in an area of heavy snowfall, or if you desire to place heavy furniture or planters on your deck.

Wood is the most economical material to use for deck construction and will be the only one described here. You will have to use a wood that is naturally resistant to decay such as redwood or cedar, or pressure treated woods. For the latter use penta-treated wood for the posts, and wood treated with water-borne salts for all wood above the soil which could come in skin contact. Be sure that treated wood has been treated under pressure to ensure that every cell is saturated with the preservative. Most lumberyards will certify the wood to that effect. Wood which has merely been dipped into a preservative or brushed with it will not resist decay. Several metal items are necessary for building decks such as including nails, bolts, screws, beam and joist hangers, post anchors, and so forth. These metals should be hot-dipped galvanized (cadmium plated in the case of bolts and screws), or primed and painted to minimize rusting. Rusting nails and metal parts stain wood and eventually lose their strength and holding power. The main components of a deck include footings, posts, beams, joists, planking, railing, and steps. The components are assembled in about that order as well. The footings are below the frost line and bear the weight of the deck, supported further by the soil under the footings. The vertical support from the top of the footing to the bottom of the deck is the post. Attached to the post or placed on top of it comes the beam. Joists are placed on top of the beam unless the beams are spaced close enough together so joists are not needed. The horizontal planking which forms the surface of the deck is nailed (or screwed) to the joists or beams. Next comes the railing which is needed for decks above ground to prevent people from being hurt if they fall off. The final component is steps to allow occupants of the deck to descend to a lower level if they so desire. The easiest way to determine the size and spacing of the components is to refer to the following tables. Remember that these tables are based upon rather average conditions. If your conditions are not in that category, then you should seek assistance as described earlier in this section.

Install concrete footings down at the frost line; two feet is the minimum depth for stability. They should be sized to handle the load in relation to the bearing capabilities of the soil. Consult local sources such as the Soil Conservation Service for soil information. A 16 x 16 inch square 10 inches deep is the recommended minimum for a footing. The posts are attached to the footings, and in turn support the beams. Whether you use joists depends upon your design. A low deck close to the ground may not allow sufficient room for joists. In this case place the beams closer together: they should be no farther apart than the Table shows for the spacing of planking. This would mean that the beams would be 5 feet apart if you are using 2 x 4 southern yellow pine planking, or 42 inches for 2 x 4 redwood.

For upper-level decks, where the space below is going to be used as a patio or for other recreational purposes, a minimum number of supporting beams and posts is desirable. Use joists to distribute the load of the deck to the smaller number beams and posts.

Space deck boards (planking) 1/8 to 1/4 inch apart for drainage. The deck can be flat, but if tongue and groove planking or marine plywood is used, you will need to slope the deck to provide drainage.

Table 7.4 — Minimum beam sizes and spans[1]

Species group[2]	Beam size (in.)	Spacing between beams[3] (ft.)								
		4	5	6	7	8	9	10	11	12
1	4x6	Up to 6-ft. spans →								
	3x8	Up to 8-ft. →		Up to 7'	Up to 6-ft. spans →					
	4x8	Up to 10'	Up to 9'	Up to 8'	Up to 7'	Up to 6-ft. spans →				
	3x10	Up to 11'	Up to 10'	Up to 9'	Up to 8'	Up to 7'	Up to 6-ft. spans →			
	4x10	Up to 12'	Up to 11'	Up to 10'	Up to 9'	Up to 8'	Up to 7'	Up to 6-ft. spans →	Up to 6-ft.	
	3x12		Up to 12'	Up to 11'	Up to 10'	Up to 9-ft.	Up to 8'	Up to 7-ft.	Up to 7-ft. spans	
	4x12			Up to 12-ft.	Up to 11'	Up to 10'	Up to 10-ft.	Up to 8-ft. spans	Up to 8-ft. spans	
	6x10				Up to 12'	Up to 11'	Up to 11'	Up to 10-ft. spans	Up to 9-ft.	Up to 9-ft.
	6x12						Up to 12-ft. spans		Up to 10-ft. spans	
2	4x6	Up to 6-ft. →								
	3x8	Up to 7-ft. →		Up to 6-ft. →						
	4x8	Up to 9'	Up to 8'	Up to 7'.	Up to 6-ft. spans →					
	3x10	Up to 10'	Up to 9'	Up to 8'	Up to 7-ft.	Up to 6-ft. spans →				
	4x10	Up to 11'	Up to 10'	Up to 9'	Up to 8'	Up to 7-ft. spans →	Up to 6-ft. spans			Up to 6'
	3x12	Up to 12'	Up to 11'	Up to 10'	Up to 9'	Up to 8-ft.	Up to 7-ft. spans →			
	4x12			Up to 12'	Up to 11'	Up to 10-ft.	Up to 9'	Up to 9-ft. spans →		
	6x10				Up to 11'	Up to 10-ft.	Up to 9-ft.		Up to 8-ft.	
	6x12					Up to 12-ft. spans		Up to 11-ft.		Up to 10'
3	4x6	Up to 6'								
	3x8	Up to 7'	Up to 6'							
	4x8	Up to 8'	Up to 7'	Up to 6-ft. spans →						
	3x10	Up to 9'	Up to 8'	Up to 7'.	Up to 6-ft. spans →					
	4x10	Up to 10'	Up to 9'	Up to 8'	Up to 7'	Up to 6-ft. spans →		Up to 6-ft. spans	Up to 6-ft.	
	3x12	Up to 11'	Up to 10'	Up to 9'	Up to 8'	Up to 7-ft. spans				
	4x12	Up to 12'	Up to 11'	Up to 10'	Up to 9'	Up to 8'		Up to 6-ft. spans	Up to 7-ft. spans	
	6x10				Up to 9-ft.				Up to 7-ft.	Up to 6'
	6x12				Up to 11-ft.			Up to 10-ft.		Up to 8'

[1]Beams are on edge. Spans are center to center distances between posts or supports. (Based on 40 p.s.f. deck live load plus 10 p.s.f. dead load. Grade is No. 2 or Better; No. 2, medium grain southern pine.)

[2]Group 1 — Douglas fir-larch and southern pine; Group 2 — Hem-fir and Douglas-fir south; Group 3 — Western pines and cedars, redwood, and spruces.

[3]Example: If the beams are 9 feet, 8 inches apart and the species is Group 2, use the 10 ft. column; 3×10 up to 6-ft. spans, 4×10 or 3×12 up to 7-ft. spans, 4×12 or 6×10 up to 9-ft. spans, 6×12 up to 11-ft. spans.

USDA Handbook No. 432

159

Table 7.5 — Maximum allowable spans for deck joists[1]

Species group[2]	Joist size (inches)	Joist spacing (inches)		
		16	24	32
1	2x6	9'-9"	7'-11"	6'-2"
	2x8	12'-10"	10'-6"	8'-1"
	2x10	16'-5"	13'-4"	10'-4"
2	2x6	8'-7"	7'-0"	5'-8"
	2x8	11'-4"	9'-3"	7'-6"
	2x10	14'-6"	11'-10"	9'-6"
3	2x6	7'-9"	6'-2"	5'-0"
	2x8	10'-2"	8'-1"	6'-8"
	2x10	13'-0"	10'-4"	8'-6"

USDA Handbook No. 432

[1]Joists are on edge. Spans are center to center distances between beams or supports. Based on 40 p.s.f. deck live loads plus 10 p.s.f. dead load. Grade is No. 2 or Better; No. 2 medium grain southern pine.

[2]Group 1 — Douglas-fir-larch and southern pine; Group 2 — Hem-fir and Douglas-fir south; Group 3 — Western pines and cedars, redwood, and spruces.

Table 7.6 — Maximum allowable spans for spaced deck boards[1]

Species group[2]	Maximum allowable span (inches)[3]					
	Laid flat				Laid on edge	
	1 x 4	2 x 2	2 x 3	2 x 4	2 x 3	2 x 4
1	16	60	60	60	90	144
2	14	48	48	48	78	120
3	12	42	42	42	66	108

USDA Handbook No. 432

[1]These spans are based on the assumption that more than one floor board carries normal loads. If concentrated loads are a rule, spans should be reduced accordingly.

[2]Group 1 — Douglas-fir-larch and southern pine; Group 2 — Hem-fir and Douglas-fir south; Group 3 — Western pines and cedars, redwood, and spruces.

[3]Based on Construction grade or Better (Select Structural, Appearance, No. 1 or No. 2).

Table 7.7 — Minimum post sizes (wood beam supports)[1]

Species group[2]	Post size (in.)	Load area[3] beam spacing x post spacing (sq. ft.)									
		36	48	60	72	84	96	108	120	132	144
1	4x4	Up to 12-ft. heights ————→				Up to 10-ft. heights→		Up to 8-ft. heights →			
	4x6					Up to 12-ft. heights ———→				Up to 10-ft→	
	6x6									Up to 12-ft→	
2	4x4	Up to 12-ft.→		Up to 10-ft. hts. ——→		Up to 8-ft. heights ————→					
	4x6			Up to 12-ft. hts. ——→		Up to 10-ft. heights ——→					
	6x6					Up to 12-ft. heights ————→					
3	4x4	Up to 12'	Up to 10'→		Up to 8-ft. hts. ——→			Up to 6-ft. heights ———→			
	4x6		Up to 12'→		Up to 10-ft. hts. ——→			Up to 8-ft. heights ———→			
	6x6				Up to 12-ft. heights ——————————→						

USDA Handbook No. 432

[1]Based on 40 p.s.f. deck live load plus 10 p.s.f. dead load. Grade is Standard and Better for 4- × 4-inch posts and No. 1 and Better for larger sizes.

[2]Group 1 — Douglas-fir-larch and southern pine; Group 2 — Hem-fir and Douglas-fir south; Group 3 — Western pines and cedars, redwood, and spruces.

[3]Example: If the beam supports are spaced 8 feet, 6 inches, on center and the posts are 11 feet, 6 inches, on center, then the load area is 98. Use next larger area 108.

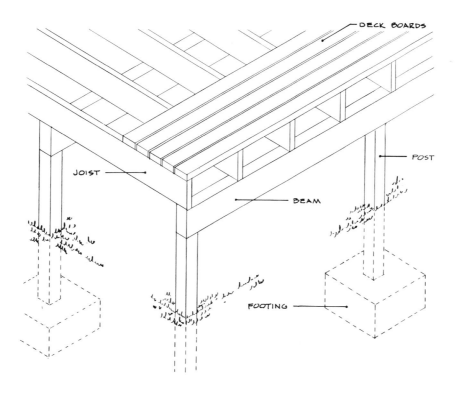

Fig. 7.104 *Common components of most decks.*

Fig. 7.105 *A deck for many functions. Design by Arthur W. Erdfeldt.*

Fig. 7.106 *The mesh railing is ideal for small children. Design by Blair and Zaik.*

162

Fig. 7.107 *Planters and water add much to this deck.*

Fig. 7.108 *The bench serves as a railing and provides seating as well.*

163

Fasteners

Nails are the most commonly used fasteners and are the least expensive and easiest to use; however, they have the poorest holding power and fail or pull out in most stress conditions. Spirally grooved nails or nails with deformed shanks hold the best but may not always be available with a rust-resistant coating. Nails should be long enough to penetrate the receiving member by a minimum of 1-1/2 inches, unless the member is thinner than 1-1/2 inches. A 10 penny nail is the maximum size for holding together two 2 x 4s. A 16 penny nail provides good holding power if you are nailing 2 x 4 deck boards flat to a 4 x 8. Where splitting may occur predrill to three-fourths the diameter of the nail. Two nails per joint is recommended for 2 inch deck boards 4 and 6 inches wide laid flat; three nails per joint is needed for wider boards. Use screws, lag screws, and bolts for railings, steps, and benches — anywhere impact and movement are involved. There are three types of screws; flat, oval, and round headed. Screws should be long enough to penetrate the receiving member by a minimum of 1 inch; predrilling to three-fourths of the screw diameter is necessary to prevent splitting. Flat and oval-headed screws are best for the most exposed situations because they protrude the least and are less likely to scratch, snag clothing, or become uncomfortable to sit on the touch.

Use lag screws to fasten large members where bolts cannot be used. Predrill holes to three-quarters of the diameter of the screw, and place a washer under the screw head. If the screws are used for seats or railings that are 2 or more inches thick, countersink them so the head is flush with the surface. Bolts are the best fasteners because they provide the best rigidity. There are two types of bolts: carriage, with a rounded head, and machine. Carriage bolts are best for areas that will come in contact with human skin, but they are the hardest to remove later because it is so difficult to get a wrench on their heads. Drill holes the same diameter as the bolts, and insert washers under the heads and nuts. As a rough guide, 1/4 inch diameter bolts can be used for 2 to 3 inch members, 3/8 inch bolts for 3 to 6 inch member, and 1/2 inch bolts for 4 inch and larger wood members. Use a minimum of two staggered bolts per joint, increasing to three or more for members 6 inches or larger.

Other metal fasteners that can be used in decks (or shelters) include steel pipe flanges, post flanges, T cleats, straps, angles, and beam hangers. Several ways these fasteners can be used are illustrated.

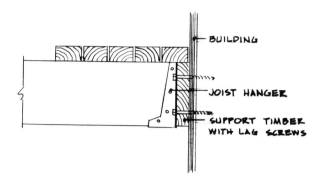

Fig. 7.109 *Detail for using a joist hanger.*

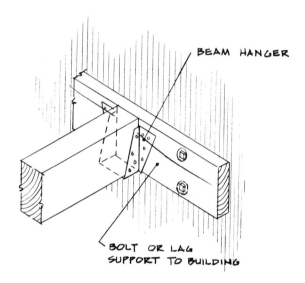

Fig. 7.110 *Detail drawing for a beam hanger.*

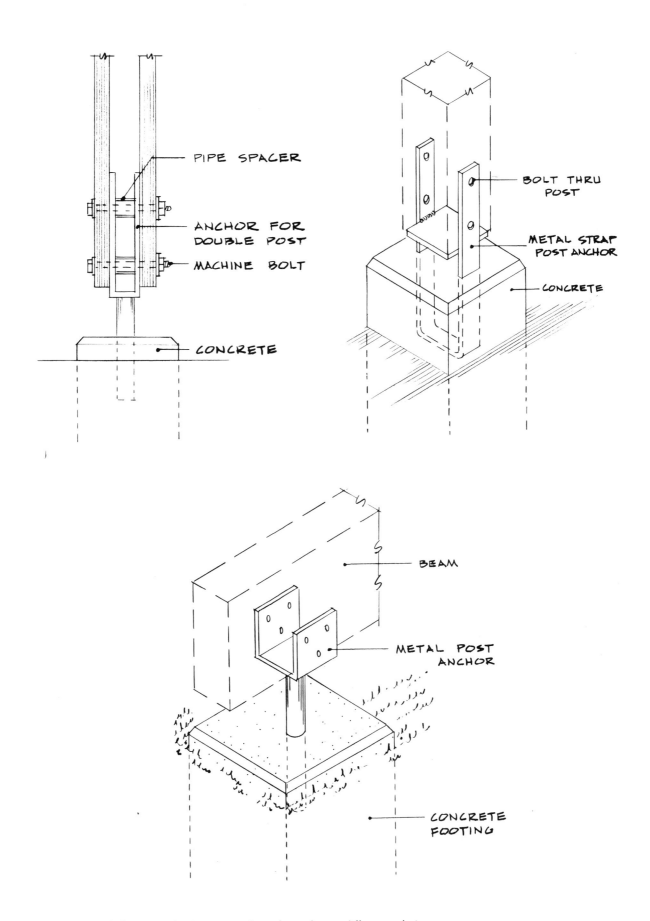

PIPE SPACER

ANCHOR FOR DOUBLE POST

MACHINE BOLT

CONCRETE

BOLT THRU POST

METAL STRAP POST ANCHOR

CONCRETE

BEAM

METAL POST ANCHOR

CONCRETE FOOTING

Fig. 7.111 *Details for post to footing connections, three of many different techniques that can be used.*

165

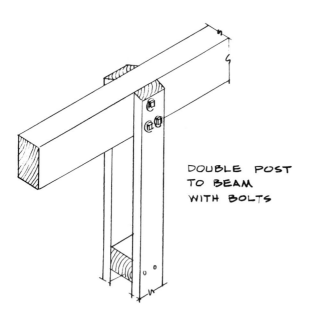

DOUBLE POST
TO BEAM
WITH BOLTS

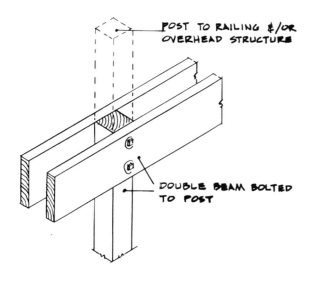

POST TO RAILING &/OR
OVERHEAD STRUCTURE

DOUBLE BEAM BOLTED
TO POST

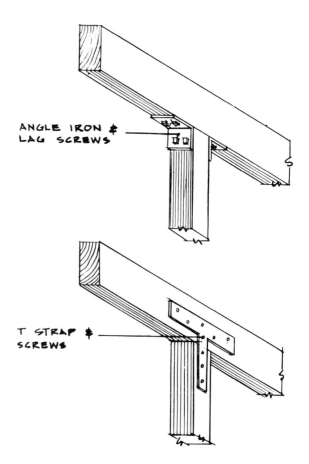

ANGLE IRON &
LAG SCREWS

T STRAP &
SCREWS

Fig. 7.112 *Details for post to beam connections.*

Bracing

Decks or other structures that stand free (independent) of adjacent structures have to be braced to prevent unwanted movement. You can use 2 x 4s for braces less than 8 feet long and 2 x 6s for those longer than 8 feet. Fasten braces with bolts or lag screws.

Railings

Generally a railing is not needed for low decks or structures; check you local building codes for exact requirements. Some codes require minimum railing heights of 36 inches when any deck is 48 inches or higher above grade. There are several design possibilities for railings, as illustrated. However, several standards have to be followed. The railings should be rigid and capable of supporting at least 20 pounds per square foot of lateral load. Posts should not be more than 6 feet apart to support a 2 x 4 rail and should be attached as part of the structure and extend through the deck boards and be attached to the beams. Use fasteners other than nails (except for the intermediate rails), screws are the best. For the safety of children, there should be no opening larger than 3 1/2 inches, thus the bottom rail should not be higher than 3 1/2 inches above the deck, and verticals should not be further than 3 1/2 inches apart. Typically a child cannot get its head through this narrow opening.

Benches are a nice feature of decks which you can combine with railings for additional function. Integrally design and construct support members to joists and extend them up through the decking, or attach fabricated steel straps attached to the surface of the deck.

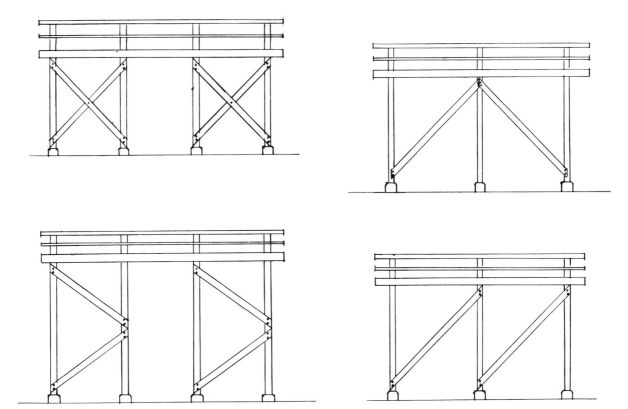

Fig. 7.113 *Different methods for bracing deck posts.*

Fig. 7.114

Fig. 7.115 *Design by Walker Harris Associates, Inc.*

Fig. 7.109 - 7.116 *Three of many different possible railing designs.*

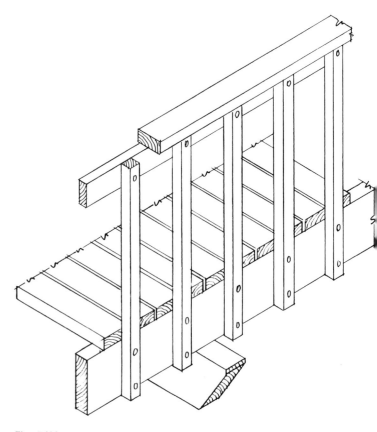

Fig. 7.116

Stairs and Steps

Wood stairs generally use stringers and treads. Stringers can be 2 x 10s or 2 x 12s attached to the deck and to a firm base, preferably concrete. Two stringers can support treads up to 48 inches wide, except for Group 3 wood species, which are limited to 42 inches if you are using 2 x 4s laid flat. Notch the stringers to hold the treads, or attach cleats, which are stronger because the stringer remains at full size. Nails are not recommended on stairs, use screws. A railing is not absolutely necessary when one or two steps are used for low decks, but they are handy for elderly or handicapped persons. The height of the railing is the same as discussed under the section of steps.

The riser-tread relationship may be somewhat steeper than for other outdoor use, but risers should not be higher than 7 inches. For comfort, the product of a riser-tread relationship should total between 72 and 75. For example, a 7-inch riser multiplied by the tread has to equal 72 to 75. Thus, to figure the tread for a 7-inch riser; the tread should thus be 10-1/2 inches (using 75). For a 6-1/2 inch rise, the tread should be (selecting 73) between 11-1/4 to 11-1/2 inches. A 2 X 12 is 11-1/4 inches wide and would be one choice for use as a tread. Two 2 x 6s with a 1/4-inch space would total 11-1/4 inches.

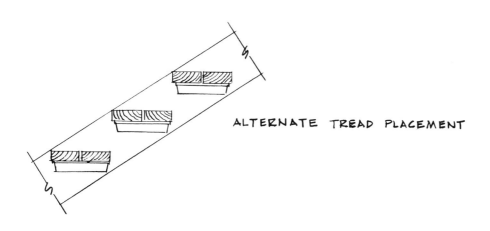

ALTERNATE TREAD PLACEMENT

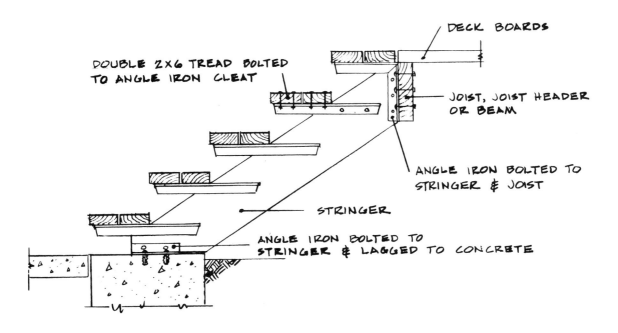

DECK BOARDS

DOUBLE 2X6 TREAD BOLTED TO ANGLE IRON CLEAT

JOIST, JOIST HEADER OR BEAM

ANGLE IRON BOLTED TO STRINGER & JOIST

STRINGER

ANGLE IRON BOLTED TO STRINGER & LAGGED TO CONCRETE

Fig. 7.117 *Details for wood steps.*

Fig. 7.118

Fig. 7.119

Fig. 7.120

Fig. 7.118 - 7.120 *Handrails for steps, three of many different design possibilities.*

170

Fig. 7.121 *A gazebo designed by Germano Milono.*

SHELTERS

Shelters (gazebos, arbors) and overhead structures can be open, providing partial or temporary shade, or roofed, for permanent protection from the sun and rain. The components, joining techniques, bracing, and so on for shelters are similar to those used for decks. Because of wind and/or snow loads, the loading for most areas of the country is the same as for decks, so the tables can be used for selecting component sizes. If you live in an area that gets very little if any snow and only slight wind, you might be able to use smaller components or components spaced further apart, but you should consult with a professional first (see Appendix A).

There are many different design possibilities for roofs. The roof can be an open structure, providing little shade but interesting shadow patterns, or it can support vines (like a trellis or arbor) or temporary canvas panels. It can be flat or sloped, partially open with closely spaced wood strips, or completely solid. If you want something other than the simple overhead structures illustrated here, you will need assistance with truss roofs and so forth from a local professional.

Fig. 7.122 *Wood and fabric shelter.*

Fig. 7.123 *Overhead structure which is relatively open and lets the sun shine through. Good for drier climates. Design by Ned Rucker.*

Fig. 7.124 *Oriental style shelter with a deck overlooking a pond.*

Fig. 7.125 *Oriental shelter made of snow fencing supported by a beam and two steel poles. Design LaPorte County Landscaping.*

Fig. 7.126 *Arbors can be built to support vines and provide summer shelter.*

Fig. 7.127 *Shelter at the end of a swimming pool providing 50% shade. Design by Walker Harris Associates Inc.*

Fig. 7.128 *A small octagonal shelter can serve as a retreat, a place of quiet and solitude.*

Fig. 7.129 *Structure with vines provides a pleasant lounging space adjacent to a swimming pool. Landscape design by Barbara J. Ziolkowski.*

BENCHES

Permanently installed and constructed benches can be quite functional yet attractive. There are many different styles and types you can build: simple, flat, and backless structure, those with backs for better support, benches that are free standing or attached to walls, or part of a raised planter. Also several manufacturers produce ready-made benches that can be easily installed.

Benches are most comfortable when they are 16 to 18 inches above the ground. If a bench has a back, you can slope the horizontal surface of the bench slightly backward, creating a slight angle that will make the bench more comfortable. A preferable horizontal surface for sitting is one at least 18 inches wide and deep flat benches wider than 18 inches are ideal around swimming pools for sunbathing because people can lay on them.

Wood benches are warm to the touch. Stone and concrete benches, although they fit nicely into the design by virtue of their color, texture, and appearance, are cold to sit on except during the hottest part of the summer when the sun is shining.

Fig. 7.130

Fig. 7.131

Fig. 7.130 - 7.134 *A few of the many ways benches can be designed.*

Fig. 7.132

Fig. 7.133

Fig. 7.134

POOLS, PONDS, AND FOUNTAINS

Water has considerable aesthetic appeal. Whether splashing in a fountain or lingering in a quiet pond, water can be a focal point within a particular landscape design.

To effectively plan, you must consider the cost of adding water into the landscape design, long-term maintenance costs, and other problems. You have to frequently clean pools and fountains to remove the dirt, leaves, and debris that accumulates almost daily. Algae may grow and discoloration from iron and other chemicals that accumulate within the pool or on the fountain structure and equipment can occur. Water used in shallow situations rapidly evaporates and thus will have to be replaced. Water in fountains is most economically recirculated by an electrical pump, but energy costs can make this a problem.

If you live in an area where freezing occurs, you should drain your pool or fountain in the winter. (Unfortunately this exposes the structural portions of the pool or fountain and looks unattractive.)

A swimming pool can be an integral part of the landscape if you carefully work with a reputable installer to select a shape and design that will fit the rest of the garden design. Most swimming pools must conform to Board of Health and building code regulations.

Most pools and water features may be viewed in some areas as attractive nuisances — a danger to small children — and thus must be fenced. (see Appendix B for a reference providing additional technical information.)

Aesthetics

In nature water is either fairly still (ponds and lakes) or moving (waterfalls, rushing mountain streams, or slowly meandering rivers). In a landscape design natural and contrived effects can be created. The quiet water can be duplicated in reflecting pools, which may be structural in character, such as rectangles or circles, or in natural earthen ponds. Moving water can be cascading, moving from one level to another, straight, pulsating, aerated, bubbling, jetting from simple orifices, or any combination of these effects. By adding programmed timing controls, you can create various effects of a few minutes or hours duration, and additional lighting will provide nighttime visual appeal. But besides imparting delightful sights and sounds, pools, ponds, and fountains can serve other purposes. For example, a pool may complement a piece of sculpture, or the water may reflect natural or structural scenic views, such as trees, a home, a well-designed garden, or a shelter. Natural ponds can be wildlife or fishing areas or holding ponds to contain water and prevent it from surging downstream after heavy storms. The sound effects from some water features can mask irritating nearby noises, such as traffic on roads or highways.

Natural Ponds

Natural ponds can be constructed in any number of different physical situations. The easiest type to build and maintain is one formed by excavating into a natural water table. You will have to provide a form of erosion control like sod or riprap along the edges. For the water in a natural pond to be free of stagnation, 50 percent of the surface of the pond should be 6 feet or deeper. Some movement of water through the natural table will add to the pond's water quality. If you build a shallower pond, you can minimize stagnation by using floating jets or other types of forced circulation.

When ponds are created in natural drainage areas, such as along an intermediate stream bed, they depend upon surface drainage as a source to fill the pond. Depending upon the soil, you may have to treat the bottom of the pond to prevent seepage. You can add chemicals to clay soil to bind the soil particles together and prevent water movement through them. Other possibilities include installing concrete, asphalt, or plastic membranes to seal the bottom of the pond. Your local conservation agent may be helpful as a source of information on designing and building natural ponds.

Professional Assistance

Because of the structural complexity of many water features as well as the plumbing and electrical work required, you should secure the services of an experienced design professional (see Appendix A).

Fig. 7.135 *Pool and fountain containing a wood sculpture.*

Fig. 7.136 *Quiet reflecting pool. Smooth black pebbles lining the bottom create a sense of depth and increase the reflectivity. Design by Frits Loonsten.*

Fig. 7.137 *A splashing fountain can be used in combination with a swimming pool to increase the visual and sound appeal of water.*

Fig. 7.138 *A waterfall, imitating nature, can be constructed of varying size boulders. Design by Wimmer Yamada Associates.*

Fig. 7.139 *A natural rock waterfall incorporating several water related plants.*

SPRINKLER IRRIGATION SYSTEMS

When plastics came on the market several years ago, sprinkler manufacturers began to produce sprinkler heads, pipes, fittings, and so on made of plastic. This breakthrough enabled homeowners to install their own systems rather than hiring a plumber. Many different types and styles of plastic sprinkler heads are available and these vary from manufacturer to manufacturer; consult local sources such as hardware, and farm supply stores for the availability of sprinkler heads and other equipment. Space and install the system according to the recommendations of local dealers. Most manufacturers produce sprinkler heads that have a center section which pops up when the unit is in operation to distribute water without interference from blades of grass and retracts when the water stops flowing. This makes it possible to easily install the head flush with the grass and prevents the lawn mower from cutting or clipping off the head. Other special devices include bubbler heads for watering small areas adjacent to the house where you do not want the spray to hit, or shrub beds where flood irrigation is more desirable than spraying a lot of water. This is particularly true for such plants as roses, where water on their leaves may encourage mildew and other diseases.

You can buy simple electrical timers and electric valves that automate the irrigation system; the system can then provide water to the lawn, shrubs and flowers when you are away. (Figures 7.140 to 7.141)

If your irrigation system is in an area subject to freezing, slope the sprinkler lines to facilitate draining. The drain valve can be either manual or automatic. Put a small pocket of gravel (about 1 cubic foot) around the valves to absorb water and to quickly evacuate the pipe and prevent any freeze damage to it or any of the sprinkler equipment.

Sprinkler distribution systems in shady areas should be valved separately from those on the sunny south and west exposures because the more exposed locations will dry out faster and thus will need more water. Separating the systems will prevent excessive drying in exposed areas or excessive wetting in shady areas. When too much water is used in shady areas, some plants such as yews may drown or an excessive formation of moss and other undesirable characteristics will occur.

If you are connecting sprinkling system to an existing valve or outlet above ground level, you can do so without professional assistance. However if you want to connect to your city water line between the meter and the place where the line enters your house you will need to get the assistance of a plumber who can make the connection and install a backflow

Fig. 7.140 *Electronic irrigation timer controls up to 8 valves. Courtesy of The Toro Co.*

Fig. 7.141 *A group of 3 electric irrigation valves in a valve box. Courtesy of The Toro Co.*

Fig. 7.142 *A twelve-inch pop-up sprinkler head allows water to spray out over flower beds and ground covers. Courtesy of The Toro Co.*

prevention valve which is required in order to prevent any bacteria or pollution from your lawn or yard from flowing back into the city water system should the water be shut off for any reason. If you connect to an existing valve or hose bib above ground level this backflow prevention device should also be installed. (See Figures 3.27 and 3.28 for a sample irrigation plan and details.)

Drip Irrigation

As supplies of water around the world become increasingly scarce, this method of irrigation is gaining in popularity. This type of irrigation involves the slow application of water directly to the root zone of the plant. It uses a special head or outlet called an emitter. Water may be released by the emitter drop by drop or a slow trickle. Drip irrigation systems are easier to install and are less expensive. Because

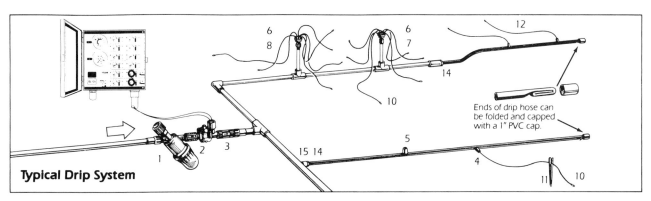

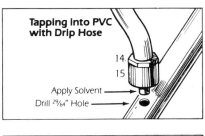

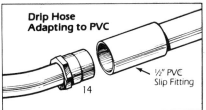

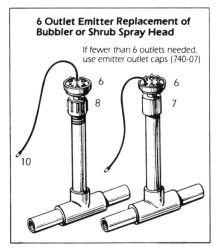

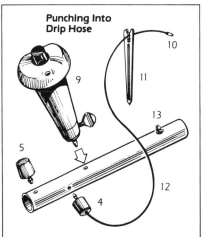

Fig. 7.143 *Components for a typical drip irrigation system: (1) Filter, (2) Automatic valve, (3) Pressure regulator, (4) Emitter, (5) Emitter, (6) 6-outlet emitter, (7) Micro-tubing, (8) Micro-tubing, (9) Hole punch, (10) Insect cap, (11) Micro-tube stake, (12) Micro-tubing, (13) Mistake or goof plugs, (14) Compression adapter, (15) Tapered pipe adapter. Courtesy of The Toro Co.*

of the slow application of water, runoff is virtually eliminated and nearly all of the water soaks into the soil around the root zone of the plant where it is most needed. Evaporation is nearly eliminated as no water is sprayed into the air as with conventional irrigation systems. There is less weed growth because less surface area of the soil is watered. (see Appendix B for a reference providing additional technical information.)

OUTDOOR LIGHTING

Lighting can extend the usefulness and enjoyment of the outdoors by adding several hours to the normal daylight hours. Lighting can also increase safety at night and add to the overall aesthetic values and attractiveness of the homesite.

Whereas daytime lighting will light the entire site, nighttime lighting can create certain compositions. For example, you can accent fences, fountains, sculpture, or specimen plants. The lighting can be overhead, low-level front or back, or spot lighting. Many different techniques are possible to achieve different effects.

Several manufacturers produce fixtures in many different styles. For evening outdoor activities, low-level lighting can be used for relaxation and dining as well as for general lighting. A higher level of lighting is necessary for reading and active participation in sports such as volleyball, badminton, or croquet. Safety lights can discourage intruders, and walks and driveways can be lighted to safety guide family and guests, preventing nighttime accidents and making pedestrian movement easier on steps, walks and slopes. You can use a timer to be sure certain outside areas are always lit when you want them to be and eliminate the bother of manually turning the lights off and on. New electronic timers can be programmed to vary the timing — a useful practice to discourage intruders. For intruders you might also consider installing a passive infra-red sensor which turns lights or other devices (i.e. a horn) on when a warm-bodied object moves through the detention pattern. When the intruder is scared away the unit shuts itself off after a short period of no motion.

Lighting can be just as dramatic in the winter as in the summer. Light fixtures that illuminate a multiple trunk of a tree will look just as interesting on a winter night as during the summer, and if there has been a wet snow, the winter scene may well be more dramatic at night than in the day. And water, whether in a reflecting pool or moving in a splashing fountain, can be extraordinary with the proper lighting. Amber light in water provides a sense of warmth; blue lighting produces a cool effect that is

Fig. 7.144 *Emitter irrigating a newly planted Lantana.*

especially attractive to those living in warmer climates. It is possible to use changing colors, but sometimes this can impart a circus effect rather than the restrained, subdued effect that is more desirable in home environments.

Four Guidelines for Lighting

You can create shadows against wall surfaces or across paving, but they need to be carefully controlled because shadows can be rather weird looking or overly dramatic if not carefully handled. Trees and shrubs with unusual foliage or interesting shapes can be accent lighted. Those with a rather artistic character are more interesting than those that are a solid mass of foliage or uniform in appearance. Use indirect lighting where possible to emphasize the color and texture of the surface; direct lighting can produce a rather flat, uninteresting lighted form.

Some variation in lighting is desirable. Subdued, small amounts of light in nearby areas contrast nicely with farther areas than receive increasing amount of light. Do not completely flood areas with light; highlight some areas, but leave others almost totally dark, to create greater interest. Thus it is better to use several light fixtures than one very powerful one. The color of the light can produce different effects. White light provides the greatest illumination for the amount of electricity being used, and it is very useful for patio areas and areas where games are being played. For a warmer effect for nearby areas, use reds, yellows, and ambers, which provided dramatic effects in water. However, they

Fig. 7.145 *Down lighting with low fixtures along a garden path.*

Fig. 7.146 *Redwood low voltage light provides soft light along an entrance walk.*

tend to make foliage look rather uninteresting, whereas green or blues have a better effect on foliage. Blue used in the background for backlighting can be very dramatic and create a sense of depth or make the garden look larger than it really is. Blues can also be used for creating moonlight effects. Combinations of lights within the garden area can produce warmth close at hand, with yellow or ambers and blue in the background to create depth.

Light Level

The amount of light needed for illumination is typically measured in footcandles. Footcandle is a unit of measure that is the amount of light cast on a surface one foot square from a standard candle one foot away.

A well-lit room will have from 70 to 150 footcandles. A small desk lamp may emit about 30 footcandles. On a sidewalk below a street lamp the light might be measured around .3 footcandle. Full moonlight measures about .1 footcandle. Effective garden lighting can range from .5 to 5 footcandles. Illumination higher than 5 might create complications with glare or interference with neighbors. Most garden fixtures provide illumination in the 3 to 5 footcandle range.

Equipment

There are essentially two choices of fixtures: those that operate on 110 volts, and those that operate at a low voltage, usually 12 volts. You can easily install low-voltage lighting and run the wiring across the ground without burying it. However, most low voltage is suitable only for low-level lighting applications and subtle effects; it is not practical to use low voltage lighting for dining, reading, or illuminating a play area. Lighting with 110 volts is better for most activities, but it must be installed by a licensed electrician — the hazards of miswiring are too great for the untrained person.

Initially you may want to buy a few fixtures and run extension cords from a house outlet, temporarily placing fixtures in different locations to determine the kinds of effects you want. The permanent fixtures should be installed by an electrician.

While the electrician is on the job, you may want to consider more water proof outlets. Additional circuits can be run easily at the same time and waterproof outlets can be established anywhere in the garden for temporary additional lighting needed from time to time; for example, Christmas lighting, play activities, weddings, fountain recirculation pumps, or for cooking on the patio or in the garden area. Follow the manufacturer's recommendations for the wattage of bulbs to fit into your fixtures. Bulbs smaller than those recommended can be used

Fig. 7.147 *Mushroom lights and Christmas lights are used along this set of steps.*

Fig. 7.148 *Fluorescent fixture inside handrail provides non-glare economical lighting for steps. Design by Edward Durrell Stone.*

without difficulty, and may in fact need to be used to balance the lighting. If uniform light is needed along any particular area, and more than one color of bulb is being used, remember that bulbs with dark color coatings such as red or blue, yield far less total light than white, so red or blue bulbs have to have considerably more wattage than a white bulb. In other words, you may have to use colored bulbs with maximum wattage but a white bulb with much less wattage to create a balance. Most building codes now require that outdoor circuits be connected to a ground fault interrupter (GFI). This particular unit, even though somewhat expensive, ensures that if a fault develops anywhere along the grounding system, it will shut off the power automatically so an accidental shock will not occur.

You must also consider timers, which enable outdoor lighting to be regularly turned on at sunset and off later at night. Photocells turn lights on automatically in the evening and off at dawn, if you want lights on all night for safety. These photocells also relieve you of the task of turning lights on and off, use power more efficiently, and ensures that lights will be operational whenever you are away during the evening or on vacation. You may want to also consider the anti-intruder sensor described

Fig. 7.149 *Uplighting the trunks of trees for emphasis.*

Fig. 7.150 *Fixture detail for Fig. 7.149.*

Fig. 7.151 *Light bark trees with multi-trunks are especially attractive when night lighted.*

Fig. 7.152 *Downlights placed in trees should be attached with spring clips and cushioning to reduce damage to the bark and allow expansion as the tree grows. Their effects can be seen in Figures 7.153 and 7.154.*

Fig. 7.153 *Backlighting of tree trunks.*

Fig. 7.154 *Carefully placed lighting creates a pleasant evening dining environment.*

186

Fig. 7.155 *Down lighting adds much to ultimate garden detail and spaces.*

Fig. 7.156 *Backlighting of shrub highlights the brick wall.*

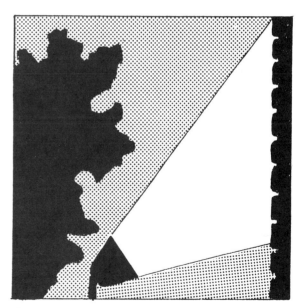

Fig. 7.157 *Fixture detail for Fig. 7.156.*

Fig. 7.158 *Lighting of a waterfall adds nighttime excitement.*

Fig. 7.159 *Lights places in pool, front of rock, in the rock, and against the fence behind planting create a feeling of depth as well as many light and shadow patterns.*

188

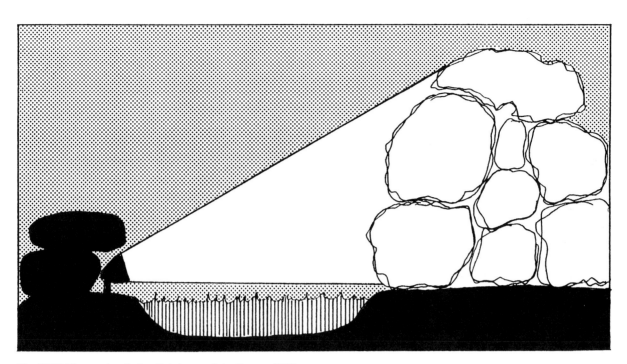

Fig. 7.160 *Fixture details for lighting rock in Figures 7.158 and 7.159.*

earlier in this section. Where fluctuating light levels are needed, plan on a dimmer, which lights the area when people want to read or play vigorously and lowers the light level for more relaxing day or night activities. (see Appendix B for a reference providing additional technical information.)

PLAY AREAS AND EQUIPMENT

The area set aside for small children to play in can be simple, with just a small sandpile, to something more elaborate, such as a ready-made piece of equipment sold by a local supplier or an item you designed and built. Simple sand areas have to be enclosed to keep the sand from moving beyond its boundaries. Drill holes in timbers and then put 1/2 x 30-inch steel reinforcing rods through the holes (as illustrated for retaining walls and steps elsewhere). The sand area can be recessed if the drainage is good; if the soil drains poorly, the sand should be above the surface so the water can drain away from the top. Sand has the disadvantage of attracting cats and their resulting litter, which is not desirable. To protect the sand from the animals, put a cover over the top of the sand area. An alternative to sand, one that is not attractive to cats is shredded hardwood bark. This is perhaps more useful in play areas where children need a cushion to absorb accidental falls.

A ready-made swing or slide is generally fine, but check the safety features. There is a lot of inexpensive equipment on the market and much of it is poorly designed and of short durability. Be sure the equipment is sturdy and well anchored to the ground so it will not move, and be sure no parts can pinch children or inflict other injuries that might occur through misuse or even normal use of the equipment. Most equipment should be galvanized or painted with a plastic or enamel coating to make it durable. All joints and moving parts should be designed for long-term wear with a minimal amount of attention, ensuring that over time a bolt or swivel will not break and cause a child to fall to the ground.

With a little imagination you can create play things that are very durable and exciting to children. Materials that will be in contact with children's skin and yet need to last a long time have to naturally decay resistant, such as redwood or cedar, or pine or fir treated with one of the metallic salts such as chromated copper arsenate. The pine or fir will look green, but is safe so long as a child does not eat the wood. Warning: any materials treated with creosote or pentachlorophenol will be toxic to children's skin.

Insert posts into the ground at least to the depth of the frost line; pour concrete around the post to make sure it is securely anchored. Bolts should be tightened periodically to ensure that the joints remain tight, if they come lose they may cause an accident. All metal parts should be galvanized or zinc plated to prevent rusting.

Fig. 7.161 *Swing, slide and crawl-through-pipe are the dominant activities in this play area constructed with wood poles.*

190

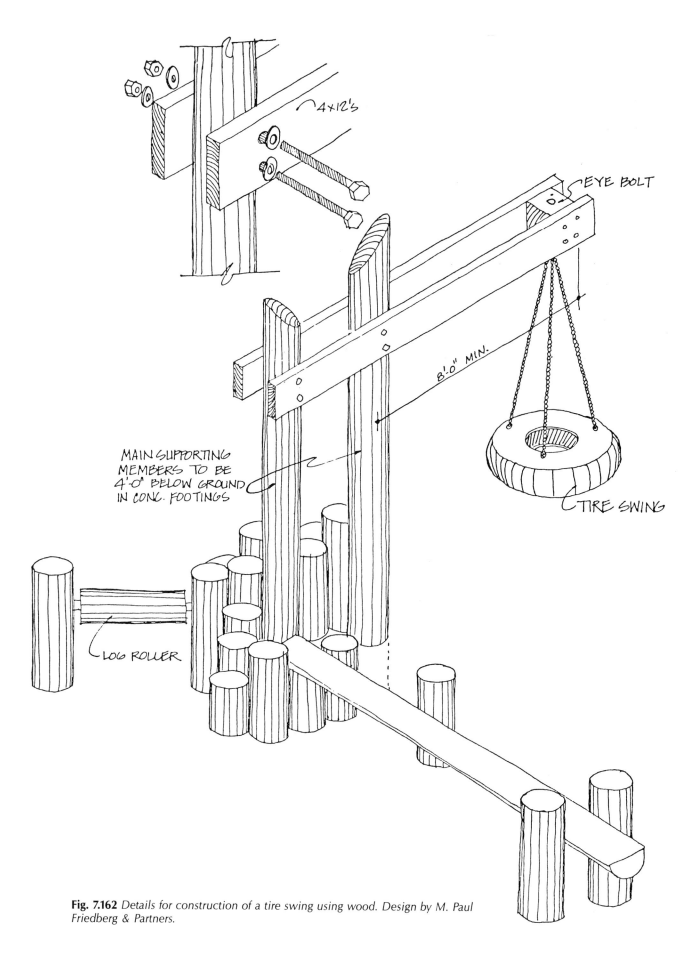

EYE BOLT

4×12'S

8'-0" MIN.

TIRE SWING

MAIN SUPPORTING
MEMBERS TO BE
4'-0" BELOW GROUND
IN CONC. FOOTINGS

LOG ROLLER

Fig. 7.162 *Details for construction of a tire swing using wood. Design by M. Paul Friedberg & Partners.*

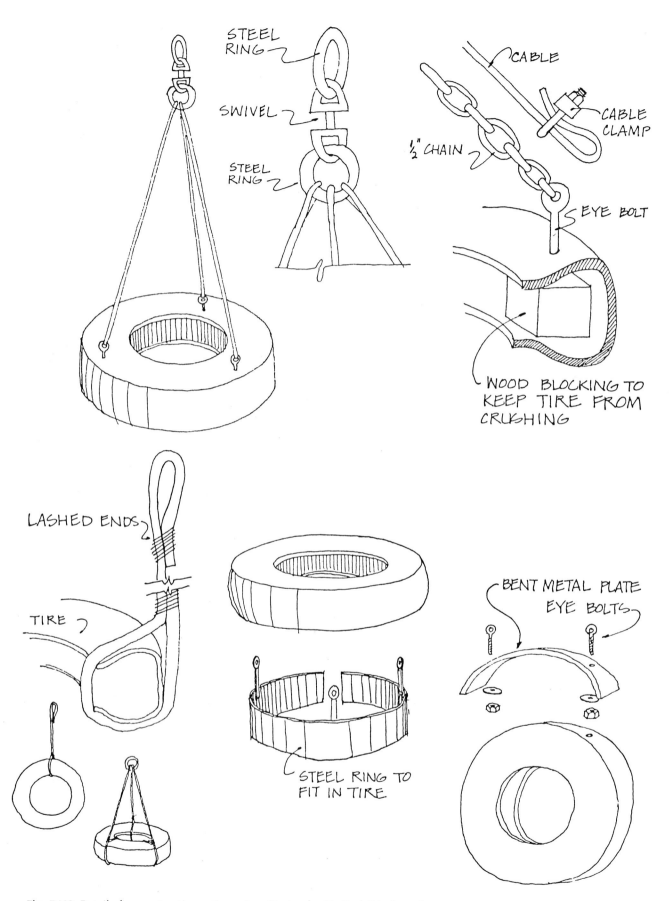

STEEL RING

SWIVEL

STEEL RING

CABLE

CABLE CLAMP

½" CHAIN

EYE BOLT

WOOD BLOCKING TO KEEP TIRE FROM CRUSHING

LASHED ENDS

TIRE

STEEL RING TO FIT IN TIRE

BENT METAL PLATE EYE BOLTS

Fig. 7.163 *Details for constructing a tire swing. Design by M. Paul Friedberg & Partners.*

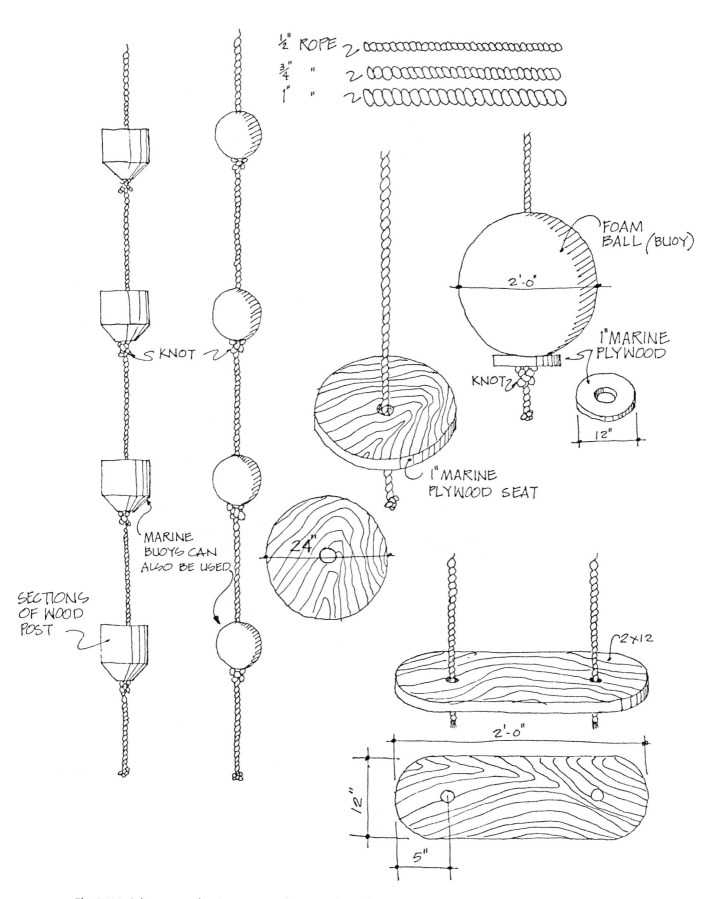

Fig. 7.164 *Other types of swings. Design by M. Paul Friedberg & Partners.*

193

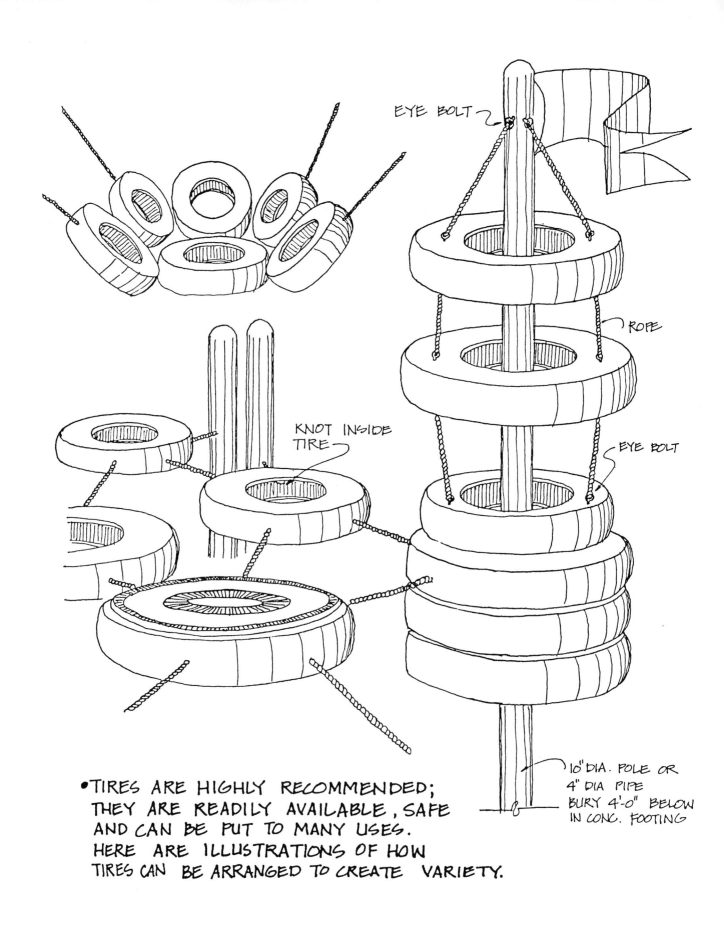

EYE BOLT

ROPE

EYE BOLT

KNOT INSIDE TIRE

10" DIA. POLE OR 4" DIA PIPE BURY 4'-0" BELOW IN CONC. FOOTING

•TIRES ARE HIGHLY RECOMMENDED; THEY ARE READILY AVAILABLE, SAFE AND CAN BE PUT TO MANY USES. HERE ARE ILLUSTRATIONS OF HOW TIRES CAN BE ARRANGED TO CREATE VARIETY.

Fig. 7.165 *Using tires in a variety of ways. Design by M. Paul Friedberg & Partners.*

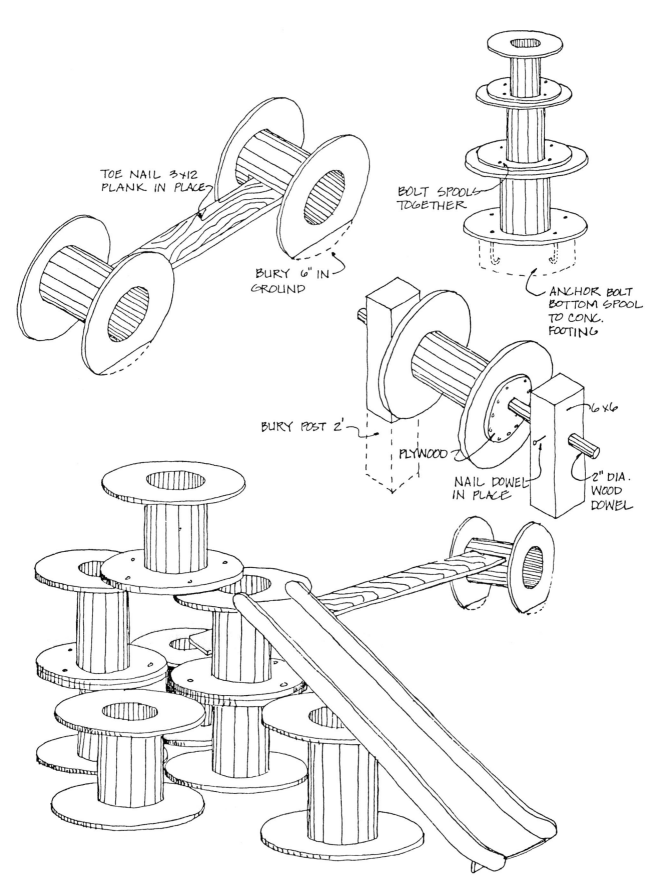

TOE NAIL 3×12 PLANK IN PLACE

BURY 6" IN GROUND

BOLT SPOOLS TOGETHER

ANCHOR BOLT BOTTOM SPOOL TO CONC. FOOTING

BURY POST 2'

PLYWOOD

NAIL DOWEL IN PLACE

6×6

2" DIA. WOOD DOWEL

Fig. 7.166 *Using spools discarded by telephone and power companies. Design by M. Paul Friedberg & Partners.*

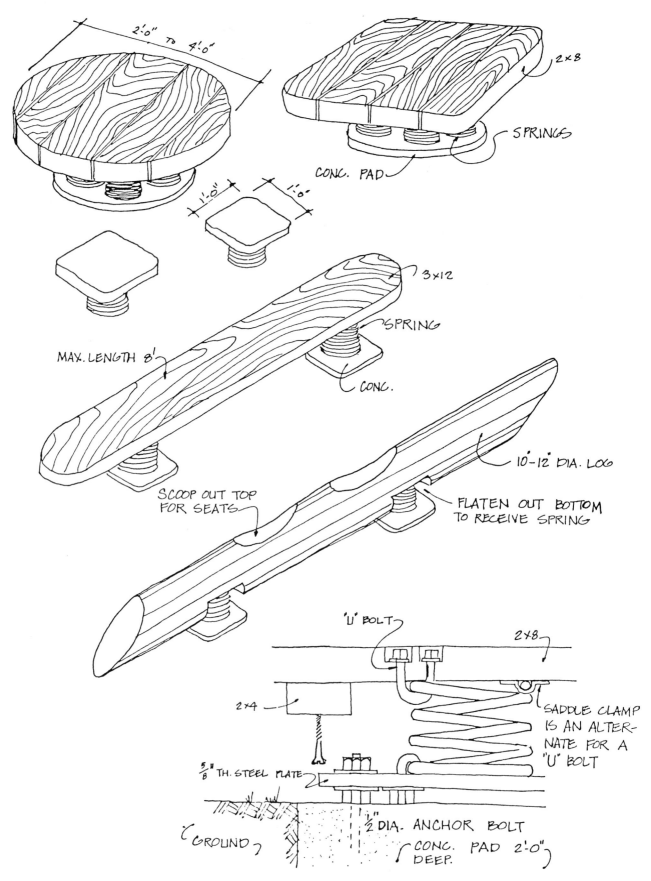

Fig. 7.167 *Details for the construction of spring pads. Design by M. Paul Friedberg & Partners.*

Fig. 7.168 *Play space can be accommodated just about anywhere. In the evening the wood panel can be replaced hiding the play space, keeping cats out, and increasing usable patio space for entertaining.*

PLANTERS AND POTS

Small portable planters offer the home-owner an opportunity to build an item and gain experience working with wood at a relatively small expense. Planters and pots can add color to the patio when planted with flowers and can be moved about to create different effects. They can be used as a focal point of green or brighter colors, and are especially useful to landscape difficult spots that otherwise might look drab.

Planters and pots require more care than plants at ground level because the soil dries out faster. The restricted root zone results in the slower growth of plants, and if planters are not properly drained plants can be drowned.

PLANTS AND PLANTING

Once the hard materials are in place, the soil can be prepared and the plants installed. Included in the planting installation phase may be trees, shrubs, ground covers, flowers and lawns. Volume II of this book describes the proper planting methods to ensure that your landscaping will thrive and look its best. The author of Volume II is Dr. Philip L. Carpenter of Purdue University's Department of Horticulture.

If you have existing trees on your site, you will learn how to protect them during construction. One chapter will help with the 'how' and 'where' of buying plants. The proper techniques for staking, mulching, pruning and fertilizing new plantings are explained. Selecting the best grass varieties for your particular area and general lawn care is the subject of still another chapter.

When your planting is installed, maintenance becomes important for the survival and health of your landscape. If you have concern about keeping maintenance to a minimum you should consult Volume II before completing your design. The physical care of plants includes watering, fertilizing, pruning, pest management and weed control.

Should you decide that you will need some help to do some or all of your landscape installation, a chapter on how to hire and work with a contractor is included in the appendix of Volume II.

CONCLUSION

This book has provided you with an overview of the planning, design and construction phases of residential landscaping. It does not contain all the answers because there are so many variables, but hopefully the principles and guidelines will be helpful and you will be able to achieve a satisfying and functional landscape.

Fig. 7.169 *A planter can be a focal point in a garden design.*

Fig. 7.170 *Redwood planter.*

Fig. 7.171 *Redwood planter.*

Fig. 7.172 *Small planter sculptured from stone.*

Fig. 7.173 *Fiberglass planter containing cactus and other arid climate plants.*

Appendix A

Selecting the Landscape Architect and How to Work With Him/Her

WHAT IS A LANDSCAPE ARCHITECT?

Most Landscape Architects are trained to design and create outdoor living environments, and their services extend far beyond designing with plants. Their training is somewhat parallel to that of architects and engineers. Whereas the architect may have been trained to design buildings and an engineer to handle the structural design or utilities involved with a building, the landscape architect has been trained to plan those areas outside of the building. Sometimes the services of these professionals tend to partially overlap, because of the interrelationship that a building has with its site. It is therefore important that these professionals cooperate and work togetether.

If you are considering selecting a site and hiring an architect to design your home, it would be well to consider selecting the landscape architect before the purchase of a site and having him coordinate closely with the architect during the design and planning of your home.

Because of his unique training and background in botany, geology, ecology, meteorology, and construction, he is able to evaluate a site in terms of your wants and needs, and make recommendations. He can assist the architect in placing the house on the site to provide the best orientation to the sun, and desirable views, and to relate the house to the future activities that may take place on the site based upon your needs. If you are uncertain about identifying and formulating your needs, your Landscape Architect can assist you with this phase.

If there are existing trees or other plant materials on the site which you have selected for your home he can make recommendations for the protection of these materials, and will quickly be able to visualize how these fit into the future design of the landscape.

Most landscape architects have been trained to understand grading and drainage, which somewhat parallels the work of a civil engineer. This understanding helps him to aid the architect to properly place the house on the site to make sure that water run-off goes in the right directions, that it does not adversely affect future use areas of the site, and does not flood or drown plants which are to be saved and utilized in the new design.

One of the basic differences between the landscape architect and the work of an architect is this: whereas the house is built in a matter of weeks, and will appear complete, the landscape, upon completion, will be small and immature. It will require years before it will begin to show forth the full beauty and quality of design. Thus, the work of a landscape architect does not show its full character in the beginning but requires time for it to be completed.

If you do not feel that you can afford the professional services of a landscape architect and an architect in selecting your site, designing your home and planning the future landscape, the alternative is to select your own site based upon some of the recommendations in this book, select a contractor who can build a house based upon your selected plans, or plans which he provides, and then proceed with the development of your own landscape design. The process for planning your own design is discussed in Chapter 3 of this book.

FINDING A LANDSCAPE ARCHITECT

Should you decide to use the professional services of a landscape architect to design the landscaping of your home, the following suggestions for finding and selecting him might be helpful.

If you have selected an architect to design your home, he might be able to provide a list of landscape architects he knows that you can contact. He may be willing to recommend those with whom he prefers to work closely, though many consistently work with only one.

Another source may be friends or home-owners in the neighborhood who may have previously utilized the services of landscape architects.

The yellow pages of your directory can be a source of finding landscape architects, though not all landscape architects are listed there. The background, abilities, and qualifications of the landscape architects that are listed vary considerably. We will discuss why this is so a little later.

Another means of locating landscape architects is to write to the American Society of Landscape Architects, 4401 Connecticut Ave. N.W., Washington, D.C. 20008. They will generally be willing to send you a list of the landscape architects within your state. Since not every landscape architect is a member of this organization, the list will not represent all the landscape architects which may be available in your area.

Because some landscape architects may not be listed in the yellow pages or as a member of the American Society of Landscape Architects (ASLA), you can locate some of these by contacting local governmental park departments, either city, county, regional, or state and recreation departments, city planning, area planning, county planning agencies where landscape architects might possibly be employed. There are many instances where landscape architects employed full-time for governmental agencies enjoy preparing residential landscape designs as an after hours or evening work activity. It serves to provide them with design opportunities not available to them in their regular line of employment and in many cases it provides an additional source of income. Some nurseries employ a landscape architect as part of their operations. Indeed, some large nurseries will have more than one in a special design section of their company. Not every individual is equally qualified, trained, or experienced, and it will require some investigation on your part to insure that the individual that you select can perform the functions you expect of him.

SELECTING THE LANDSCAPE ARCHITECT

It is well to spend some time determining the qualifications of the landscape architect which you are about to hire. He should have been trained in a curriculum of landscape architecture and received at least a Bachelor's Degree with a minimum of four years of schooling. The school from which he graduated should have been accredited by the Landscape Architecture Accreditation Board of the American Society of Landscape Architects.

In addition to this, some states require the licensing or professional registration of landscape architects. If your state is one of these, this additional qualification should be required. In some states, however, untrained landscape architects have been able to become licensed or registered under a "Grandfather Clause." The qualification of licensing alone may therefore not be sufficient to qualify a landscape architect to design for you, if he has not taken an examination.

After licensing has been established in a state, a young professional seeking a license is required to take a comprehensive examination to determine his competence. This exam is usually the Uniform National Exam (UNE) prepared by the Council of Landscape Architectural Registration Boards which represents most states that require licensing. Nearly all states require a period of apprenticeship or internship under the direction of a licensed landscape architect to insure a minimum of practical experience before licensure.

After establishing these basic qualifications, interview each of your candidates to determine their personality characteristics and how well you might be able to develop a working relationship with each of them. Review with them the nature of their services, what they will charge you for the services that you have decided you want him to perform. It is also very helpful for you to review some of the projects which the landscape architect that you are interested in may have designed previously. If the landscape architect is willing, you may be able to get him to name a few clients which he has served, and in this way you may look at the projects he has designed and interview his previous clients to see how well he performed.

SERVICES OF A LANDSCAPE ARCHITECT

Just as an architect prepares drawings for the construction of a house, so the landscape architect also prepares drawings and specifications for all of the facilities which may be constructed as part of the landscape. In addition to trees, shrubs and flowers, he may also prepare plans for paving, patios, and sidewalks, and any structures such as a deck or gazebo, fences, walls, pools or fountains, grading, drainage, etc.

If you have done a good job of determining the qualifications of your landscape architect and interviewing him you will have established a good working relationship, and you will have communicated to him a thorough outline of your landscape needs: outdoor living areas, your recreation facilities needed, storage and utility needs, a listing of favorite plants that you would like to see incorporated into the design. Any special needs such as a dog run, vegetable garden, or a swimming pool should also be made known. Based upon your needs, upon the characteristics of the site as he has analyzed it, and the nature and character of your home, he will then prepare a preliminary proposal of how he perceives your needs and how he conceives the creation of a landscape design. You should have an opportunity to review with him his proposals and okay them before the preparation of the final drawings and specifications which will be used to go to bid, that is, secure prices from several contractors.

A reputable landscape architect will be in a position to recommend contractors and nurseries which can carry out your landscape design. Your landscape architect may have recommended, and you may have agreed, to utilize his services in observing and checking the progress of the work during construction to make sure that his design is completely carried out using quality materials installed to the satisfaction of his specifications.

Very early in your relationship with the landscape architect he should be aware of any budget limitations which you might need to impose on the project. If your budget is quite tight, you should consider the possibility of having your landscape architect develop a master plan for the entire development of your site and then recommending year by year phasing of the work with either a contractor or yourself installing the project over a longer period of time. Even though this will not give you an immediate, finished landscape design, the utilization of a master plan for a long-range development will spread your costs over a longer period of time, and you can still achieve the total design to satisfy your needs. A checklist appears in Chapter 2 to help you think through your needs and evaluate them.

FEES AND CHARGES

The Landscape Architect may charge for his services in any one of three different ways: 1) a flat fee, 2) a percentage of the construction fee, or 3) a figure in dollars-per-hour. How he charges will depend somewhat on the type of service you need and the size of the project.

When a Landscape Architect is on the staff of a nursery, a fee may be established for the preparation of plans, but the fee also may be waived if you agree to purchase the plant materials from the nursery or have the nursery construct the landscape for you. In such a situation, a Landscape Architect may or may not be influenced in his planting design by the inventory of plant materials already available in the nursery.

Those Landscape Architects who are not employed by a nursery will generally make their living entirely from the fees they charge and not receive any discounts from the suppliers of materials or services.

The flat fee is a lump sum figure, a one-time cost which generally is agreed upon by both parties in advance of any work performed. This lump sum figure may cover any or all of these services previously described such as, selecting the site, consulting with the architect of your home or any other professionals who may be involved, the design of any outdoor construction as well as the location of trees and shrubs, preparation of plans, specifications and contracts and any inspection required during construction. This type of fee is quite generally used for residential situations where the homeowner would like to know exactly what his costs are going to be at the outset of a project.

For large scale projects it is quite common for the Landscape Architect's services to be charged in a form of a fee based upon a percentage of the total contract cost of the project. Usually a budget for such a large scale project has been established or certain guidelines given to the Landscape Architect to design within. He then goes ahead in preparing the plans and specifications of contract documents, places the project out to bid to several contractors, accepts the bids, and the final contract price, if agreeable to the owner, establishes a contract then between the contractor and the owner. The Landscape Architect's fees are then based upon a percentage of that contract price, which may range anywhere between 10 to 20 percent depending upon the size of the project and the precise services rendered. Generally the higher the contract price, the lower the percentage rate.

The third fee method, that of an hourly rate, is based upon a Landscape Architect's customary charge for consultation by the hour, or occasionally on a daily rate. Most professionals maintain a time chart for all of their projects and record the hours spent on each day as a basis of watching their costs and budgeting their time. Thus they are able to very easily bill a client for the hours spent on any particular project, if this is the most satisfactory method agreeable to both parties. It is highly probable that reputable or outstanding Landscape Architects with a high reputation within the profession, will insist upon the hourly rate to remove any tight restrictions on their ability to perform the kind of services they would like to perform for you. This is especially true if the project they are doing for you is somewhat vague, no rigid budget has been established, and you are exploring a number of miscellaneous design possibilities without a definite preconceived project or result in mind. It is not too unusual for a Landscape Architect with a top reputation to attract clients who want a unique design and are willing to pay whatever costs are involved to secure complete professional service, careful consultation, and careful design that will result in a project of which they can be proud as a unique work of art designed only for them.

In the case of the flat fee method, you may be charged a portion of that flat fee as a retainer to begin the project with the balance due upon completion. If you pursue a project and you agree to a percentage fee basis, it may well be that you will be billed for a portion of the project at the time bidding is completed and the fee at that point is established with the portion of the fee due at the completion of construction and the remainder of the fee due at the end of the final inspection. If services to you by the Landscape Architect are being provided on an hourly basis, you will probably be billed monthly for the services of the previous month.

Unless you have made an agreement otherwise with the Landscape Architect, there are some costs which may not be included within the fee described above. If you request extra sets of blueprints or request changes in the plans and specifications after you have approved the originals, or necessitate any extra travel, you create extra expenses and you may be billed for these in addition to the normal fees. The charges for such things as travel or extra sets of blueprints are generally made on the basis of actual costs, whereas other changes requiring modification to plans, etc., are charged on an hourly rate.

Contracts and Agreements

After you have selected your Landscape Architect, interviewed him, and discussed your project with him and he has indicated that he is willing to be of service to you, it is well then to establish how he is going to charge you and what fees are going to be assessed for your particular project. You should not be embarrassed or think that you will embarrass him by asking him about his fees. If he is experienced and reputable, generally he will indicate to you fairly soon what kind of costs are involved with his services. It is well that you request it, if he has not already volunteered to do so, that some written agreement be prepared which establishes precisely and in sufficient detail, all of the services to be performed and how you, in turn, will pay for those services. This may be a formal contract or an agreement in the form of a letter addressed to you by the Landscape Architect on which he has signed his name and has indicated somewhere on it a place for you to approve the agreement.

Drawing and Specifications

The Landscape Architect will prepare one or more drawings which may include any of the following.

1. Site Analysis: A plan which shows property lines, drainage patterns, topographic features, rock outcroppings, existing vegetation, directions of good views, if any, existing utilities and easements, etc.

2. Site Plan: Locates the house on the site, layout of walks, drives, parking, fences, drainage, utilities, and most other landscape features.

3. Construction Details: Specific drawings which show how steps, walls, fence, walks, pools, decks, etc., are to be built.

4. Planting Plan: The location, size and name of each plant to be installed.

5. Irrigation Plan: The location of each sprinkler head, control value, drain and sizes of pipes.

In addition he will generally prepare a written set of specifications which describe in considerable detail the quality of materials and workmanship required.

If several qualified contractors are available in your area, your landscape architect may suggest competitive bidding as a means of securing the best price possible for your landscape development project.

203

Appendix B

Technical Data
And References
For Further Reading

Aurand, C. Douglas, 1986. *Fountains and Pools.* New York: Van Nostrand Reinhold. 168 pages.

Friedberg, M. Paul, 1975. *Handcrafted Playgrounds.* New York: Random House. 123 pages.

Jackson, A., and Day, D., 1978. *Tools and How to Use Them.* New York: A. Knopf. 352 pages. (An illustrated encyclopedia of hand and power tools—their history, what they are used for, how to operate and maintain them.)

Melby, Pete, 1988. *Simplified Irrigation Design.* New York: Van Nostrand Reinhold. 190 pages.

Readers Digest, 1972. *Practical Guide to Home Landscaping.* Pleasantville, New York: Readers Digest Association. 479 pages.

Robinette, Gary O., 1972. *Plants, People, and Environmental Quality.* Washington, DC: USGPO. 137 pages.

Sunset Books. Menlo Park, California: Lane Publishing Co. (This publisher produces several paperback books containing simple and practical landscape projects for the homeowner to build.)

Walker, Theodore D., 1985. *Plan Graphics,* 3rd edition. New York: Van Nostrand Reinhold. 235 pages.

Walker, Theodore D., 1985. *Planting Design.* New York: Van Nostrand Reinhold. 151 pages.

Walker, Theodore D., 1986. *Site Design and Construction Detailing,* 2nd edition. New York: Van Nostrand Reinhold. 506 pages.

APPROXIMATE WEIGHTS OF MATERIALS

Soil, Etc.	lbs. per cu. ft.
Clay, damp	110
Clay, dry	63
Sand or gravel, loose & dry	90-105
Sand or gravel, wet	118-120
Topsoil, loose & dry	76
Topsoil, moist & packed	96

Stone	lbs. per cu. ft.
Granite	175
Limestone & Marble	165
Sandstone & Bluestone	147
Slate	175

Concrete	lbs. per cu. ft
With stone, reinforced	150
With stone, not reinforced	144
With Perlite	35-50
With Vermiculite	25-60

Fluids	lbs. per cu. ft.
Gasoline	75
Water at 4°C.	62.4
Water, ice	56

Metals	lbs. per cu. ft.
Aluminum, cast	165
Bronze, statuary	509
Iron, cast gray	450
Iron, wrought	485
Lead	710
Steel, rolled	490

Wood (12% MC)	lbs per cu. ft
Birch & Red Oak	44
Cedar, western red	23
Douglas Fir	34
Oak, white	47
Pine, southern	29-36
Redwood	28

Masonry (with mortar)	lbs. per sq. ft.
4" brick	35
4" stone or gravel	34
6" concrete block	50
8" stone, gravel, block	58
12" stone, gravel, block	90

MAXIMUM FROST PENETRATION (inches)

AVERAGE ANNUAL DEPTH OF FROST PENETRATION (inches)

Alternate Symbols for Plants

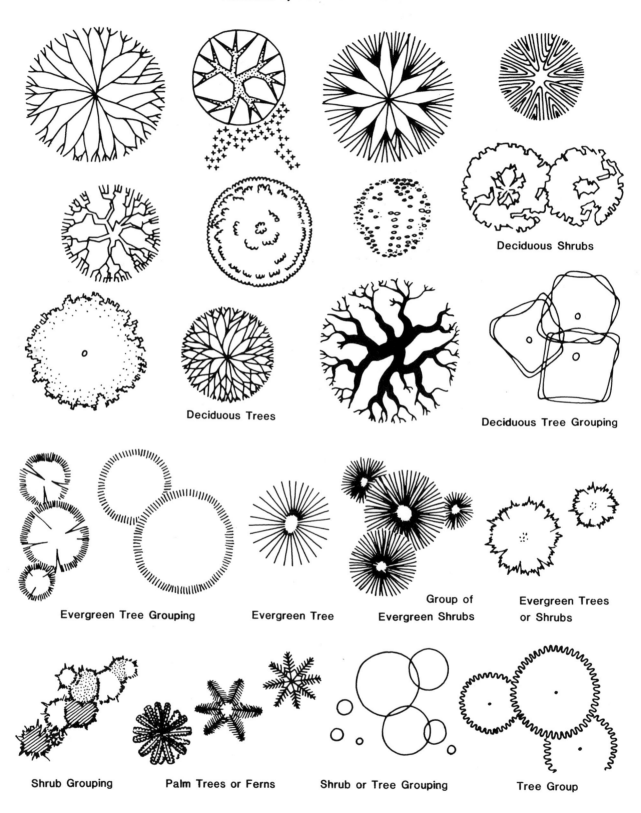

Deciduous Shrubs

Deciduous Trees

Deciduous Tree Grouping

Evergreen Tree Grouping   Evergreen Tree   Group of Evergreen Shrubs   Evergreen Trees or Shrubs

Shrub Grouping   Palm Trees or Ferns   Shrub or Tree Grouping   Tree Group

Symbols for Materials

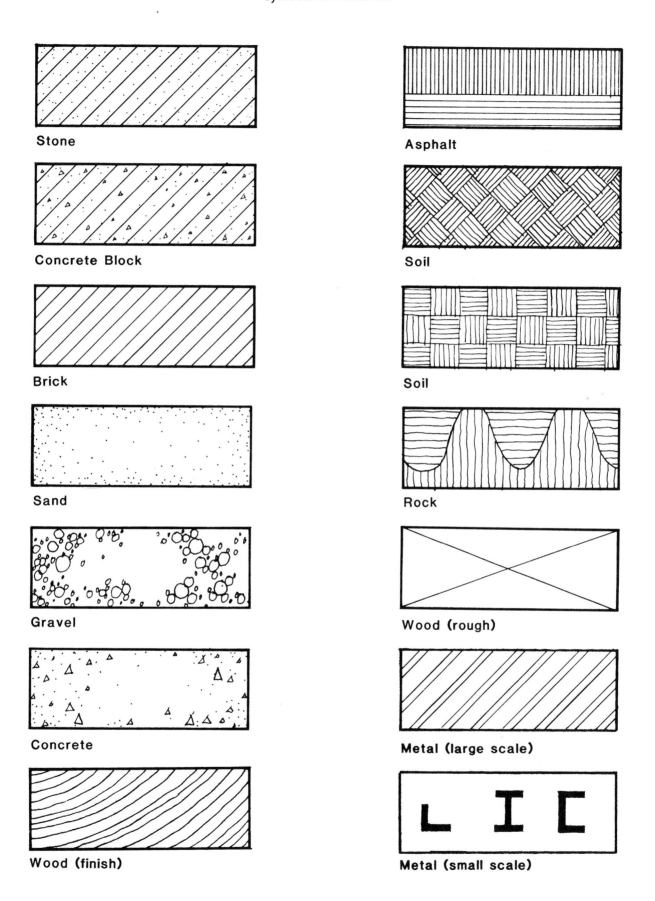

Stone

Asphalt

Concrete Block

Soil

Brick

Soil

Sand

Rock

Gravel

Wood (rough)

Concrete

Metal (large scale)

Wood (finish)

Metal (small scale)

TABLE OF NAIL SIZES

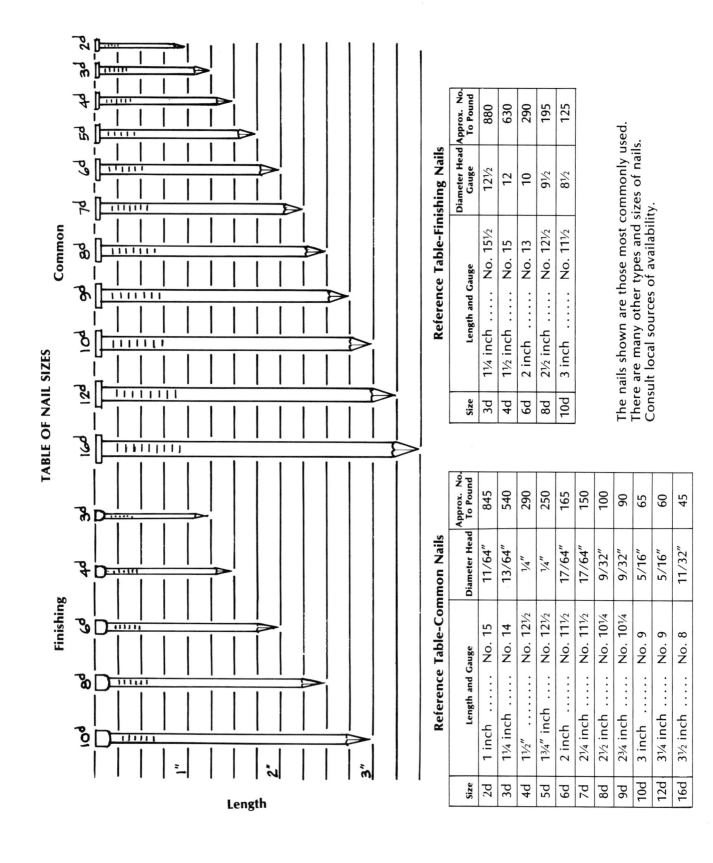

Common

Finishing

Length

Reference Table-Finishing Nails

Size	Length and Gauge		Diameter Head Gauge	Approx. No. To Pound
3d	1¼ inch	No. 15½	12½	880
4d	1½ inch	No. 15	12	630
6d	2 inch	No. 13	10	290
8d	2½ inch	No. 12½	9½	195
10d	3 inch	No. 11½	8½	125

The nails shown are those most commonly used.
There are many other types and sizes of nails.
Consult local sources of availability.

Reference Table-Common Nails

Size	Length and Gauge		Diameter Head	Approx. No. To Pound
2d	1 inch	No. 15	11/64″	845
3d	1¼ inch	No. 14	13/64″	540
4d	1½″	No. 12½	¼″	290
5d	1¾″ inch	No. 12½	¼″	250
6d	2 inch	No. 11½	17/64″	165
7d	2¼ inch	No. 11½	17/64″	150
8d	2½ inch	No. 10¼	9/32″	100
9d	2¾ inch	No. 10¼	9/32″	90
10d	3 inch	No. 9	5/16″	65
12d	3¼ inch	No. 9	5/16″	60
16d	3½ inch	No. 8	11/32″	45

TABLE OF WOOD SCREWS

Shank Sizes

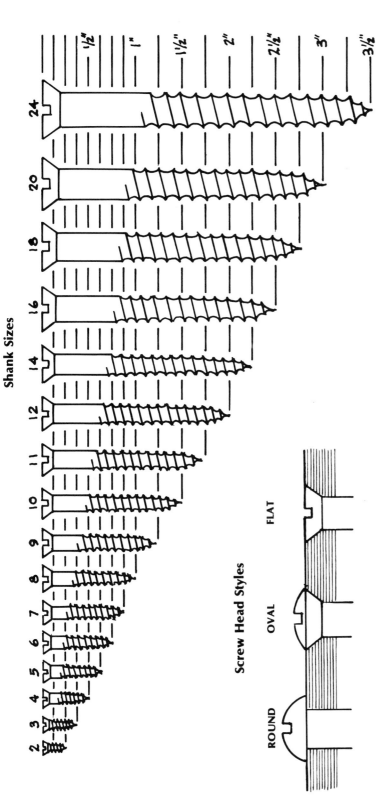

Screw Head Styles

ROUND   OVAL   FLAT

Wood Screw Length Variables

Gauge	Length
2	1/4"–3/4"
3	1/4"–1"
4	1/4"–1½"
5	3/8"–1½"
6	3/8"–2½"
7	3/8"–2½"
8	3/8"–3"
9	½"–3"

Gauge	Length
10	½"–3½"
11	5/8"–3½"
12	5/8"–4"
14	3/4"–5"
16	1"–5"
18	1¼"–5"
20	1½"–5"
24	3"–5"

Increment of length =
⅛" increments up to 1",
¼" increments from 1¼" to 3",
½" increments from 3½" to 5".

TABLE OF BOLT SIZES

CARRIAGE

Diameter	Length
1/4"	3/4"-8"
5/16"	3/4"-8"
3/8"	3/4"-12"
7/16"	1"-12"
1/2"	1"-20"
9/16"	1"-20"
5/8"	1"-20"
3/4"	1"-20"

MACHINE

Diameter	Length
1/4"	1/2"-8"
5/16"	1/2"-8"
3/8"	3/4"-12"
7/16"	3/4"-12"
1/2"	3/4"-24"
9/16"	1"-30"
5/8"	1"-30"
3/4"	1"-30"
7/8"	1 1/2"-30"
1"	1 1/2"-30"

LAG

Diameter	Length
1/4"	1"-6"
5/16"	1"-10"
3/8"	1"-12"
7/16"	1"-12"
1/2"	1"-12"
5/8"	1 1/2"-16"
3/4"	1 1/2"-16"
7/8"	2"-16"
1"	2"-16"

Increments of length =
1/4" increments up to 6",
1/2" increments up to 8",
1" increments over 8".

THICK inches	WIDTH inches	LENGTH (feet)							
		10	12	14	16	18	20	22	24
1	2	1.666	2	2.333	2.666	3	3.333	3.666	4
1	3	2.5	3	3.5	4	4.5	5	5.5	6
1	4	3.333	4	4.666	5.333	6	6.666	7.333	8
1	5	4.167	5	5.833	6.666	7.5	8.333	9.167	10
1	6	5	6	7	8	9	10	11	12
1	7	5.833	7	8.167	9.333	10.5	11.666	12.833	14
1	8	6.666	8	9.333	10.666	12	13.333	14.666	16
1	9	7.5	9	10.5	12	13.5	15	16.5	18
1	10	8.333	10	11.666	13.333	15	16.666	18.333	20
1	12	10	12	14	16	18	20	22	24
1	14	11.666	14	16.333	18.666	21	23.333	25.666	28
1	16	13.333	16	18.666	21.333	24	26.666	29.333	32
2	2	3.333	4	4.666	5.333	6	6.666	7.333	8
2	3	5	6	7	8	9	10	11	12
2	4	6.666	8	9.333	10.666	12	13.333	14.666	16
2	6	10	12	14	16	18	20	22	24
2	8	13.333	16	18.666	21.333	24	26.666	29.333	32
2	9	15	18	21	24	27	30	33	36
2	10	16.666	20	23.333	26.666	30	33.333	36.666	40
2	12	20	24	28	32	36	40	44	48

CONVERSION CHART FOR LUMBER
(changing linear feet to board feet)

.333 = 1/3   .666 = 2/3
.167 = 1/6   .833 = 5/6
.500 = 1/2

TABLES OF MEASUREMENT

Weights

English (Avoirdupois)

		Metric	
1 ton	= 2,000 pounds	1 ton	= 1,000 Kilograms
1 pound	= 16 ounces	1 kilogram	= 1,000 grams
1 ounce	= 16 drams	1 gram	= 1,000 milligrams
1 dram	= 27.34 grains		

Liquid

1 gallon	= 4 quarts	1 liter	= 1,000 milliliters
1 quart	= 2 pints		
1 pint	= 16 fluid ounces		

Length

1 mile	= 5,280 feet	1 kilometer	= 1,000 meters
1 furlong	= 40 rods	1 meter	= 100 centimeters
1 rod	= 5½ yards	1 centimeter	= 10 millimeters
1 yard	= 3 feet		
1 foot	= 12 inches		

Surface

1 square mile	= 640 acres	1 square kilometer	= 100 hectares
1 acre	= 43,560 square feet	1 hectare	= 10,000 square meters
1 square yard	= 9 square feet		
1 square foot	= 144 square inches		

MEASUREMENT EQUIVALENTS

Length

Meter	= 1.093 yards	Yard	= 0.9144 meter
	= 3.281 feet	Foot	= 0.3048 meter
	= 39.370 inches	Inch	= 0.0254 meter
Kilometer	= 0.621 mile	Mile	= 1.609 kilometers

MEASUREMENT EQUIVALENTS (Continued)

Metric (cont.)   English (cont.)

Surface

Square meter	= 1.196 square yards	Square yard	= 0.836 square meter
	= 10.764 square feet	Square foot	= 0.092 square meter
Square centimeter	= 0.155 square inch	Square inch	= 6.45 square centimeters
Square kilometer	= 0.386 square mile	Square mile	= 2.590 square kilometers
Hectare	= 2.471 acres	Acre	= 0.405 hectare

Volume

Cubic meter	= 1.308 cubic yards	Cubic yard	= 0.764 cubic meter
	= 35.314 cubic feet	Cubic foot	= 0.028 cubic meter
Cubic centimeter	= 0.061 cubic inch	Cubic inch	= 16.387 cubic centimeters
Stere	= 0.275 cord (wood)	Cord	= 3.624 steres

Capacity

Liter	= 1.056 U.S. liquid quarts	U.S. liquid quart	= 0.946 liter
	or 0.880 English liquid quart	Dry quart	= 1.111 liters
	= 0.908 dry quart	U.S. gallon	= 3.785 liters
	= 0.264 U.S. gallon or	English gallon	= 4.543 liters
	= 0.220 English gallon	U.S. bushel	= 0.352 hectoli
Hectoliter	= 2.837 U.S. bushels or	English bushel	= 0.363 hectoli
	= 2.75 English bushels		

Weight

Gram	= 15.432 grains	Grain	= 0.0648 gram
	= 0.032 troy ounce	Troy ounce	= 31.103 grams
	= 0.0352 avoirdupois ounce	Avoirdupois ounce	= 28.35 grams
Kilogram	= 2.2046 pounds avoirdupois	Pound	= 0.4536 kilogram
Metric ton	= 2204.62 pounds avoirdupois	Short ton	= 0.907 metric
Carat	= 3.08 grains avoirdupois		

CONVERSION FACTORS

When you know:	You can find:	If you multiply by:
Area		
acres	sq. feet	43,560.
acres	sq. meters	4,046.8
sq. centimeters	sq. feet	0.00108
sq. centimeters	sq. inches	0.1550
sq. feet	sq. centimeters	929.03
sq. feet	sq. inches	144.
sq. feet	sq. meters	0.0929
sq. feet	sq. yards	0.1111
sq. inches	sq. centimeters	6.4516
sq. inches	sq. feet	0.00694
sq. inches	sq. meters	0.000645
sq. meters	sq. feet	10.764
sq. meters	sq. yards	1.196
sq. yards	sq. feet	9.
sq. yards	sq. meters	0.8361
Length		
centimeters	inches	0.3937
centimeters	yards	0.01094
feet	inches	12.0
feet	meters	0.30481
feet	yards	0.333
inches	centimeters	2.540
inches	feet	0.08333
inches	meters	0.02540
inches	millimeters	25.400
inches	yards	0.2778
kilometers	feet	3,281.
kilometers	miles (nautical)	0.5336
kilometers	miles (statute)	0.6214
kilometers	yards	1,094.
meters	feet	3.2809
meters	yards	1.0936
miles (statute)	feet	5,280.
miles (statute)	kilometers	1.6093
miles (statute)	meters	1,609.34
miles (statute)	yards	1,760.
miles (nautical)	feet	6,080.2
miles (nautical)	kilometers	1.8520
miles (nautical)	meters	1,852.0
millimeters	inches	0.03937
rods	meters	5.0292
yards	centimeters	91.44
yards	feet	3.0
yards	inches	36.0
yards	meters	0.9144
Pressure		
grams per cu. cm.	oz. per cu. in.	0.5780
kilograms per sq. cm.	pounds per sq. in.	14.223
kilograms per sq. meter	pounds per sq. ft.	0.2048
kilograms per sq. meter	pounds per sq. yd.	1.8433
kilograms per cu. meter	pounds per cu. ft.	0.06243
ounces per cu. in.	grams per cu. cm.	1.7300
pounds per cu. ft.	kilograms per cu. meter	16.019
pounds per sq. ft.	kilograms per sq. meter	4.8824
pounds per sq. in.	kilograms per sq. cm.	0.0703
pounds per sq. yd.	kilograms per sq. meter	0.5425

CONVERSION FACTORS (Continued)

When you know:	You can find:	If you multiply by:
Velocity		
feet per minute	meters per sec.	0.00508
feet per second	meters per sec.	0.3048
inches per second	meters per sec.	0.0254
kilometers per hour	meters per sec.	0.2778
knots	meters per sec.	0.5144
miles per hour	meters per sec.	0.4470
miles per minute	meters per sec.	26.8224
Volume		
cubic centimeters	cubic inches	0.06102
cubic feet	cubic inches	1,728.0
cubic feet	cubic meters	0.0283
cubic feet	cubic yards	0.0370
cubic feet	gallons	7.481
cubic feet	liters	28.32
cubic feet	quarts	29.9222
cubic inches	cubic centimeters	16.39
cubic inches	cubic feet	0.0005787
cubic inches	cubic meters	0.00001639
cubic inches	liters	0.0164
cubic inches	gallons	0.004329
cubic inches	quarts	0.01732
cubic meters	cubic feet	35.31
cubic meters	cubic inches	61,023.
cubic meters	cubic yards	1.3087
cubic yards	cubic feet	27.0
cubic yards	cubic meters	0.7641
gallons	cubic feet	0.1337
gallons	cubic inches	231.0
gallons	cubic meters	0.003785
gallons	liters	3.785
gallons	quarts	4.0
liters	cubic feet	0.03531
liters	cubic inches	61.017
liters	gallons	0.2642
liters	pints	2.1133
liters	quarts	1.057
liters	cubic meters	0.0010
pints	cubic meters	0.004732
pints	liters	0.4732
pints	quarts	0.50
quarts	cubic feet	0.03342
quarts	cubic inches	57.75
quarts	cubic meters	0.0009464
quarts	gallons	0.25
quarts	liters	0.9464
quarts	pints	2.0
Weight		
grams	kilograms	0.001
grams	ounces	0.03527
grams	pounds	0.002205
kilograms	ounces	35.274
kilograms	pounds	2.2046
ounces	grams	28.35
ounces	kilograms	0.02835
ounces	pounds	0.0625
pounds	grams	453.6
pounds	kilograms	0.4536
pounds	ounces	16.0

Appendix C

References For Selecting Plants

General United States

Dirr, M. A., 1983. *Manual of Woody Landscape Plants,* 3rd edition. Champaign, IL: Stipes Publishing.

Flint, H. L., 1983. *Landscape Plants for Eastern North America.* New York: John Wiley.

Hillier Color Dictionary of Trees & Shrubs, 1982. New York: Van Nostrand Reinhold.

Johnson, H., 1973. *International Book of Trees.* London: Mirchell Beazley Publishers Ltd.

Johnson, H. and Miles, P., 1981. *Pocket Guide to Garden Plants.* New York: Simon & Schuster.

Wyman, D., 1971. *Trees for American Gardens.* New York: MacMillan.

Wyman, D., 1971. *Shrubs and Vines for American Gardens.* New York: MacMillan.

Arizona and California

Duffield, M. R. and Jones, W. D., 1981. *Plants for Dry Climates.* Tucson, AZ: H. P. Books.

Perry, R. C., 1981. *Trees and Shrubs for Dry California Landscapes.* San Dimas, CA: Land Design Publishing.

Sunset Books, 1979. *New Western Garden Book.* Menlo Park, CA: Lane Publishing.

Sutliff, D. A., 1983. *How to Choose a Plant When You Need One: A Guide for Plant Selection.* San Luis Obispo, CA: (published by the author).

(Also, see references listed under General United States)

Pacific Northwest

McClintock, E. and Leiser, A. *An Annotated Checklist of Woody Ornamental Plants of California, Oregon and Washington.* Berkeley, CA: Agricultural Sciences Publications, University of California.

(Also, see references listed under General United States)

Southeastern United States

Duncan, W. H. and Foote, L. E., 1975. *Wildflowers of the Southeastern United States.* Athens, GA: University of Georgia Press.

Halfacre, R. G. and Shawcroft, A. R., 1989. *Landscape Plants of the Southeast,* 5th edition. Raleigh, NC: Sparks Press.

Harrer, E. S. and Harrer, J. G., 1962. *Guide to Southern Trees,* 2nd edition. New York: Dover.

Martin, E. C. Jr., 1983. *Landscape Plants in Design.* New York: Van Nostrand Reinhold.

Odenwald, N. G. and Turner, J. R., 1980. *Plants for the South.* Baton Rouge, LA: Claitor Law Publishing.

Radford, A. E., Ahles, H. E. and Bell, C. R., 1968. *Manual of the Vascular Flora of the Carolinas.* Chapel Hill, NC: University of North Carolina Press.

Watkins, J. V., 1975. *Florida Landscape Plants.* Gainesville, FL: University of Florida Press.

Whitcomb, C. E., 1975. *Know It and Grow It.* Tulsa, OK: Oil Capital Printing Co.

Wigginton, B. E., 1963. *Trees and Shrubs for the Southeast.* Athens, GA: University of Georgia Press.

Workman, R., 1980. *Growing Native.* Sanibel, FL: Sanibel-Captiva Conservation Fund.

(Also, see references listed under General United States)

State Nursery Associations

Alabama Nurserymen's Association
P. O. Box 9
Auburn, AL 36830

Arizona Nurserymen's Association
444 West Camelback Road, Suite 302
Phoenix, AZ 85013

Arkansas Nurserymen's Association
P. O. Box 55295
Little Rock, AR 72225

California Association of Nurserymen
1419 21st Street
Sacramento, CA 95814

Colorado Nurserymen's Association
746 Riverside Drive, Box 2676
Lyons, CO 80540

Connecticut Nurserymen's Association
24 West Road, Suite 53
Vernon, CT 06066

Delaware Association of Nurserymen
Plant Science Dept.
University of Delaware
Newark, DE 19717

Florida Foliage Association
P. O. Box Y
Apopka, FL 32703

Florida Nurserymen's & Growers Association
5401 Kirkman Road #650
Orlando, FL 32819

Georgia Nurserymen's Association
190 Springtree Road
Athens, GA 30605

Hawaii Association of Nurserymen
P. O. Box 293
Honolulu, HI 96809

Idaho Nursery Association
1615 North Woodruff
Idaho Falls, ID 83401

Illinois State Nurserymen's Association
Springfield Hilton #1702
Springfield, IL 62701

Indiana Association of Nurserymen
202 East 650 North
West Lafayette, IN 47906

Iowa Nurserymen's Association
7261 NW 21st Street
Ankeny, IA 50021

Kansas Nurserymen's Association
Blueville Nursery, Route 1
Manhattan, KS 66502

Kentucky Nurserymen's Association
701 Baxter Avenue
Louisville, KY 40204

Louisiana Association of Nurserymen
4560 Essen Lane
Baton Rouge, LA 70809

Maine Nurserymen's Association
Plant & Soil Dept.
SMVTI, Fort Road
South Portland, ME 04106

Maryland Nurserymen's Association
2 Troon Court
Baltimore, MD 21236

Massachusetts Nurserymen's Association
715 Boylston Street
Boston, MA 02116

Michigan Association of Nurserymen
819 North Washington Avenue, Suite 2
Lansing, MI 48906

Minnesota Nursery and Landscape Assocation
P. O. Box 13307
St. Paul, MN 55113

Mississippi Nurserymen's Association
P. O. Box 5385
Mississippi State, MS 39762

Missouri Association of Nurserymen
7911 Spring Valley Road
Raytown, MO 64138

Montana Association of Nurserymen
P. O. Box 1871
Bozeman, MT 59715

Nebraska Nurserymen's Association
P. O. Box 80117
Lincoln, NE 68501

Nevada Nurserymen's Association
651 Avenue B
Boulder City, NV 89005

New Hampshire Plant Growers Association
194 Rumford Street
Concord, NH 03440

New Jersey Association of Nurserymen
65 South Main Street
Building H, Suite 3
Pennington, NJ 08534

New Mexico Association of Nurserymen
P. O. Box 667
Eslancia, NM 87106

New York Nurserymen's Association
P. O. Box 5185
Albany, NY 12205

North Carolina Nurserymen's Association
P. O. Box 400
Knightdale, NC 27545

North Dakota Nursery & Greenhouse Association
P. O. Box 2601
Bismark, ND 58502

Ohio Nurserymen's Association
2021 E. Dublin-Granville Road #185
Columbus, OH 43229

Oklahoma Nurserymen's Association
400 North Portland
Oklahoma City, OK 73107

Oregon Association of Nurserymen
2780 S.E. Harrison, Suite 204
Milwaukie, OR 97222

Pennsylvania Nurserymen's Association
1924 North Second Street
Harrisburg, PA 17102

Rhode Island Nurserymen's Association
P. O. Box 515
North Scituate, RI 02857

South Carolina Nurserymen's Association
809 Sunset Dr.
Greenwood, SC 29646

South Dakota Nurserymen's Association
3401 E. 10th Street
Sioux Falls, SD 57103

Tennessee Nurserymen's Association
P. O. Box 57
McMinnville, TN 37110

Texas Association of Nurserymen
7730 South I-H 35
Austin, TX 78745

Utah Association of Nurserymen
3500 South 9th East
Salt Lake City, UT 84106

Vermont Plantsman's Association
P. O. Box 438
Windsor, VT 05089

Virginia Nurserymen's Association
R. R. #4, Box 356
Christianburg, VA 24073

Washingston State Nurserymen's Association
P. O. Box 670
Sumner, WA 98390

West Virginia Nurserymen's Association
Route 1, Box 33
Talcott, WV 24981

Wisconsin Nurserymen's Association
Route 1, Box 377
Lake Mills, WI 53551

ACKNOWLEDGMENTS

The number of individuals who have had an influence in the preparation of this book is too numerous to list. Some are listed in the legends below the photographs throughout the book or on this page. To these and all the many other unnamed friends and colleagues, I say 'thank you!' An especial note of appreciation to Wendy Scofield and Don Teal who reviewed the first edition and provided suggestions for improvements. Wendy Scofield also supplied ideas for the book's graphics. Many of the ink sketches in the book are the work of Cathy Lambert Wells.

PHOTOGRAPHER CREDITS

Most of the photographs which are not credited below are the work of the author.

Cover: Lower left: Richard Maack Photography. Design by Steve Martino and Associates. Upper right: Design by McConaghie/ Batt & Associates.

Chapter 1
Fig. 1.1 Hedrich-Blessing
Figures 1.2 - 1.10 A. E. Bye
Figures 1.12 - 1.15 Courtesy of Western Wood Products Association
Fig. 1.16 Hedrich-Blessing

Chapter 3
Fig. 3.2 Courtesy of Theodore Brickman Co.
Fig. 3.4 Courtesy of Edward D. Stone, Jr. and Associates
Fig. 3.5 A. E. Bye
Figures 3.16 - 3.17 Courtesy of Alan Burke, New Image Industries, Inc.
Fig. 3.37 Don Normark
Figure 3.38 - 3.40 Steve Martino

Chapter 4
Fig. 4.4 Courtesy of the Bomanite Corporation

Chapter 5
Figures 5.1 - 5.2 Courtesy of Mark M. Holeman Inc.
Fig. 5.3 Bill Hedrich, courtesy of Irvin A. Blietz Organization, Evanston, Illinois
Fig. 5.5 Charles R. Pearson, courtesy of Western Wood Products Association
Fig. 5.6 Courtesy of the Theodore Brickman Co.
Fig. 5.12 Courtesy of the Theodore Brickman Co.
Fig. 5.14 Courtesy of Betonwerk Munderkingen GmbH
Figures 5.16 - 5.17 A. E. Bye
Fig. 5.20 Barbara J. Ziolkowski
Fig. 5.24 Courtesy of Mark M. Holeman Inc.
Figures 5.25 - 5.26 Courtesy of Theodore Brickman Co.
Fig. 5.27 Bill Engdahl, Hedrich-Blessing
Fig. 5.28 Hedrich-Blessing
Fig. 5.29 Courtesy of Mark M. Holeman Inc.
Fig. 5.30 Ken Molino, courtesy of California Redwood Association
Fig. 5.32 Ed Dull Photography, courtesy of Western Wood Products Association
Fig. 5.33 Charles R. Pearson, courtesy of Western Wood Products Association
Fig. 5.35 Julius Shulman, courtesy of California Redwood Association

Fig. 5.38 Hedrich-Blessing, courtesy of Theodore Brickman Co.
Figures 5.43 - 5.45 Courtesy of the General Electric Co.

Chapter 7
Fig. 7.3 Courtesy of the Bomanite Corporation
Fig. 7.5 Courtesy of Mark M. Holeman Inc.
Fig. 7.6 A. E. Bye
Figures 7.18 - 7.19 Barbara J. Ziolkowski
Fig. 7.36 Barbara J. Ziolkowski
Fig. 7.74 A. E. Bye
Fig. 7.79 Barbeau Engh, courtesy of California Redwood Association
Fig. 7.80 - 7.81 Tom Burns, courtesy of Western Wood Products Association
Fig. 7.89 Tom Burns, courtesy of Western Wood Products Association
Fig. 7.90 Charles R. Pearson, courtesy of Western Wood Products Association
Fig. 7.91 Tom Burns, courtesy of Western Wood Products Association
Fig. 7.92 Charles R. Pearson, courtesy of Western Wood Products Association
Fig. 7.93 Phil Palmer, courtesy of California Redwood Association
Fig. 7.94 Morley Baer, courtesy of California Redwood Association
Fig. 7.95 Tom Burns, courtesy of Western Wood Products Association
Figures 7.97 - 7.98 Charles R. Pearson, courtesy of Western Wood Products Association
Fig. 7.105 Courtesy of Western Wood Products Association
Fig. 7.106 Charles R. Pearson, courtesy of Western Wood Products Association
Figures 7.107 - 7.108 Courtesy of California Redwood Association
Fig. 7.121 - 7.123 Courtesy of California Redwood Association
Fig. 7.129 Barbara J. Ziolkowski
Fig. 7.134 Ed Dull Photography, courtesy of Western Wood Products Association
Fig. 7.140 - 7.142 Courtesy of The Toro Co.
Fig. 7.145 Courtesy of the General Electric Co.
Fig. 7.148 Courtesy of L & J Specialty Corp.
Fig. 7.149 Courtesy of the General Electric Co.
Figures 7.151 - 7.155 Courtesy of the General Electric Co.
Fig. 7.159 Courtesy of the General Electric Co.
Fig. 7.168 Ken Molino, courtesy of the California Redwood Association
Figures 7.169 - 7.171 Courtesy of the California Redwood Association

Index

surcharge 139
surface measurements 214
swimming pool 19, 33, 36, 39,
    178
swing 190-193
symbols
    for materials 209
    for plants 208
symmetrical 14

T
tennis 19
texture 84, 93
    of bark 86
timber 190
    edging 126
    retaining wall 129, 144
    steps 130
timer for irrigation 180
tires for play 194
topography 10
transition 92
transportation 9
traprock 48
tread 127-128, 169
tree
    bark 86
    forms 72
    staking 29
    symbols 208

U
urethane 44, 50
use
    facilities 19
    relationships 19
utilities 9

V
valves for irrigation 180
variegated plants 89
variety 91
varnish 44
vegetable gardens 12
vegetation 10
vertical
    form 70, 82
    reinforcing 131
vibrating concrete 45
video imaging 23
views 10
vines 81
vinyl 49
visual
    control 96
    screening 98
Vogley, John 154
volcanic rock 48, 143
volleyball 19

W
wall
    of stone 142
    sizes 132
    types 131
water 12
    for concrete 45
waterfall 178
weight measurements 214
weights of materials 205
wildlife habitat 112
wind
    load 171
    reduction 106
windbreaks 105
winter lighting 66
wood
    beam 165
    benches 174
    decks 158
    dimensions 42
    edging 126
    fence 147, 150
    for play 190
    gate 48
    physical properties of 40
    preservatives 43, 190
    products 41
    retaining wall 146
    screws 211
    sculpture 65, 177
    shingles 42
    steps 129-130

X
xeriscape 55

Z
Ziolkowski, Barbara J. 58,
    122-123, 173
zoning regulations 10